PRAISE FOR *A SIMPLER MOTHERHOOD*

"With *A Simpler Motherhood*, Emily helps mothers everywhere declutter far more than just their closets, and makes minimalism with young children not only worthwhile but (better yet) attainable."

—Erica Layne, author of *The Minimalist Way*

"Chronic list-makers unite! This book gave such specific and helpful examples about how to choose what to prioritize on those ubiquitous to-do lists that I find myself actually getting the most important things done first. Seems simple, but it's revolutionary!"

—Sherry Petersik, blogger at *Young House Love* and author of *Lovable Livable Home*

"In our fast-paced world, simplicity doesn't just *happen* for mothers. We have to pursue it. Emily carves out a path to do just that."

—Denaye Barahona, PhD, author of *Simple Happy Parenting* and host of the *Simple Families* podcast

"If you read one book on simplicity and motherhood, let it be this one. Like a long-time friend, Emily welcomes readers from page one with a warm hug, a knowing smile of understanding, and true compassion. Emily guides you through the twists and turns of what it truly means to live a beautiful and simple life, and finding those moments of simplicity when life seems overwhelming and messy. This is one book that you will not be able to put down, and you'll return to read over and over again."

—Lauren Tucker, blogger on *An Organized Life*

"Practical and inspiring, this book will encourage mothers everywhere to uncover the beauty of simplicity."

—Jennifer L. Scott, author of *Lessons from Madame Chic*

A SIMPLER
MOTHERHOOD

A SIMPLER MOTHERHOOD.

Curating Contentment,
Savoring Slow,
and Making Room
for What Matters Most

EMILY EUSANIO

CORAL GABLES, FL

Cover Design and Art Direction: Morgane Leoni
Cover Photo: Oleksandr /Adobe Stock

For permission requests, please contact the publisher at:
Mango Publishing Group
2850 S Douglas Road, 4th Floor
Coral Gables, FL 33134 USA
info@mango.bz

For special orders, quantity sales, course adoptions and corporate sales, please email the publisher at sales@mango.bz. For trade and wholesale sales, please contact Ingram Publisher Services at customer.service@ingramcontent.com or +1.800.509.4887.

A Simpler Motherhood: Curating Contentment, Savoring Slow, and Making Room for What Matters Most

Library of Congress Cataloging-in-Publication number: 2022930617
ISBN: (print) 978-1-64250-808-6, (ebook) 978-1-64250-809-3
BISAC category code HOM019000, HOUSE & HOME / Cleaning, Caretaking & Organizing

Printed in the United States of America.

To my four little blessings:

for being the only reasons I need to chase after a simpler,
more magical motherhood.

TABLE OF CONTENTS

FOREWORD

Fifteen years ago, I was at the highest *and* the lowest points of my life. I was newly married, had just purchased my first home, and was a new mother to the most beautiful baby girl I had ever seen. I was blessed with everything I had ever wanted in life, and at the same time, I was overwhelmed with daily *living*.

I felt like I was thrown into the deep end of a pool, suddenly realizing I had no idea how to swim. I was drowning in toys, laundry, dishes, and appointments, but most of all, I was drowning in my own expectations of motherhood and adulting in general.

I couldn't understand why other moms seemed to effortlessly manage it all, while I fell into bed each night with a longer to-do list than the one I started with that morning. I assumed I just had to work harder, but the more I tried to accomplish, the more overwhelmed I felt. I could never seem catch up, and I started to resent the beautiful life I had always wished for. I started to resent being a mother.

What I discovered with time (and a lot of trial and error) is that it wasn't "more" that fixed my problems, it was "less." I had to let go of all the things that didn't matter in order to gain all the things that did.

I simplified my life.

I let go of unused clutter, but even more than that, I let go of the unreal expectations I put on myself. I gave myself permission to take shortcuts and, dare I say, do things badly. The crazy thing is, when I gave myself permission to do things the "lazy" way, I accomplished so much more. When I stopped expecting perfection, I started seeing success in every area of my life.

Less is more. Less stuff, less work, less commitments, and less expectations all equal more happiness, more time, and more overall success. I know this sounds cliché, and I understand that this concept goes against *everything* society has ever taught us about success. We are told "if something is worth doing, it's worth doing right" and that "practice makes perfect." We are told to hustle, work harder, and earn more money so that we can buy more things. We are misled down this impossible path of over-complication and overwhelm.

You can make your own path—a simple path that you don't have to run down. A beautiful path that leads exactly where you want to go.

Just by choosing to read this book, you have already taken the first step down your brand-new path. This book is the shortcut to a simplified life that I wish I had fifteen years ago. Emily will walk you through *exactly* how to simplify every aspect of your life so that you can make space for what matters most.

–Cassandra Aarssen
Creator of Clutterbug™

INTRODUCTION:

My Simple Story

Life wasn't always so simple for me.

In fact, it was the presence of way too much of everything that encouraged me to pursue a simpler, slower motherhood—to chase after a life intentionally absent of all the extra: stuff, people, commitments, standards. I was six months postpartum and absolutely drowning in the weight of it all.

From the outside, my life looked exactly as I had dreamed it would. I was a stay-at-home mom with our beautiful son. We owned a lovely four-bedroom cape cod in one of the best school districts in the city. We drove expensive, pretty cars, owned pretty new things, and wore pretty new clothing.

And yet, I was pretty dang miserable.

We were doing our best to survive on one income, and yet we spent every penny we made. The stress rose in my chest each month as we dutifully made all the payments to our student loan debt, a mortgage payment slightly too large for our means, and credit card bills for frivolous, unnecessary purchases that we didn't need (especially on such a tight budget).

I was a floundering first-time mom. My son and I took daily trips through the Starbucks drive-through, with me ordering up a grande flat white while he nodded off for his morning nap in the car seat. I made weekly visits to Target, browsing the aisles in search of items that would make motherhood easier, better, and prettier. I spent my days glued to Google, searching for the perfect cleaning routine, the perfect sleep schedule, the perfect meal plans. And then I'd collapse at the end of the afternoon, too exhausted to cook dinner; so, I'd pick up the phone and order pizza delivery or sushi takeout instead of eating what was already right there in the fridge.

By all accounts, I had "made" it. I was living the suburban mom dream. Yet ironically, I was more unsettled and unsatisfied than I'd ever been. I was consuming and doing too much of everything. I was measuring my success by the tasks I accomplished; the schedules I followed; the projects I completed. The good days were marked by a completed to-do list, an obedient, well-dressed and well-napped baby, and a perfectly tidied home. Yet I'd go to bed at the end of the day with a sense of emptiness. Something was missing.

It was then that the voice started. At first, it was just a whisper: a gentle request to slow down, to stop the constant hustle and the relentless quest for perfect motherhood. It quietly rose, echoing through our newly redecorated halls and over the piles of unworn baby clothing, tags still attached. It urged me to listen, to change my ways, to stop focusing so intensely on how everything in my life *looked*—and to instead care more about how everything *felt*. And yet each time it rose above a whisper, I quickly quieted it back down by loading up the Amazon cart with a few more unnecessary items, reorganizing the playroom toys in color-coordinated order, or scrubbing my baseboards, intently certain that it would make everything better.

Except it didn't.

That whisper grew. It grew louder as we moved two more times in the next two years, relocating out of town and purchasing our second home in a city where we knew no one, and then as we searched for our third home the following year. It beckoned me to wave the white flag: to put down the credit card, the cleaning rag, and the to-do lists, and to find a better way to measure my worth as a mother.

And as we moved into house number three, I waited for the voice to stop. But it didn't. It continued to grow as we made grand plans for the future of our new home and the arrival of our new baby. It bounced off the empty walls of our massively outdated fixer-upper, urging me to stop planning, consuming, and controlling. It grew from a nagging call to an adamant demand, begging me to stop chasing after perfection and to start finding joy in the beauty of the motherhood right in front of me.

And it was then, when I was six months pregnant with our rainbow baby, that I finally decided it was time to listen.

— — —

Life since then has never been the same. It's changed in ways that are difficult to describe. A simpler existence has infiltrated every crevice of my days, every corner of my life. It's removed all the excess and stripped away all of the unnecessary—but somehow, all the best parts of motherhood still remain. A simpler life has removed the burdens of comparison and jealousy: the constant need to rush and to move on to the next. It's carved out an unfathomable amount of empty space in my heart, my head, and my days. And in its place, that empty space has been filled with an abundance of gratitude, joy, and contentment.

But it's not just about the stuff. It never is. You see, you can culti-vate a perfectly minimal life. You can pare down your home. You can declutter your space. You can strip away all the unnecessary things. But until you find joy in the space that remains, you'll be missing the entire point. Because what good is a simpler moth-erhood if you're not actually showing up for it?

That's where this book comes in. In the chapters to come, you'll find ways to help you navigate your way to simpler living in all the important areas—your home, your schedule, your budget, and your tasks. But it's so much more than that. I'll give you easy, actionable ways to immediately simplify all the tangible things, sure. But what's equally essential—the part I'll touch on consis-tently throughout the pages of this book—is learning to clear space in your mind and your soul, too. Here you will learn how to remove all the excess, the extra, the expectations and to-dos, and how to focus on what's truly important: the perfectly imperfect motherhood you have right in front of you, right now.

My hope is for you to find all the joy that I've been able to discover through a life with a little less of everything. There's such amazing happiness waiting for you once you make the courageous deci-sion to slow down and savor all the beautiful things motherhood brings. It's a heck of a journey, but it's your path to forge. And I promise you, a simpler motherhood is yours for the taking—if you make the effort to pursue it. Are you ready?

Good. Let's get started.

CHAPTER 1:

A Simpler Start

Here we go. You might be here hoping that I'm about to offer up the life-changing secret to a simpler motherhood. Maybe you're thinking that if you just removed all the clutter in your home and organized everything using the most efficient systems, life would magically be simpler.

I wish it were that easy.

There's a reason why you picked this book up. Maybe you've decluttered every inch of your home, only to find yourself with a basement full of donations and unused items six months later. Or you've invested in a professional organizer—or a bunch of expensive bins, containers, and labeling systems—only to find yourself constantly reorganizing the same items over and over again every few weeks. Perhaps you've finally minimized all your stuff. You've "arrived," right?

Wrong. I say that because I've been there too.

In the beginning of my journey to a simpler life, I tried countless different systems and methods to simplify and organize our stuff. I decanted every household good we owned. (Not familiar with the term decanting? Stay tuned for Chapter 5: A Simpler Kitchen.) I organized our playroom toys by category with coordinating white woven bins. I created a command center in our kitchen for every single piece of paper that required filing, I carefully stacked coordinating food storage containers in our cabinets, and I Konmari folded every clothing drawer to within an inch of its life. Yet life still felt way too complicated.

Because here's the truth: your environment is an important component of a simpler life, sure. But it won't solve all your problems. Until you clear all that clutter that swirls through your mind the minute you sit down in your perfectly minimized living room, nothing is going to change. Life may *look* a lot simpler, but it won't *feel* any simpler until you make peace with all that noise filling up your head.

WHAT REALLY MATTERS

How often do you pause? How often is there silence and space in your daily life? Most moments of the day, our minds are jumping from one thing to the next. As moms, we're on permanent autopilot, constantly adding to our to-do lists, shuffling our thoughts from tonight's dinner to the latest news clip and right onto the best ways to get our kids to sleep through the night. There's always another ding, whoosh, beep, or click lingering in the background, enticing us to hop aboard another train of thought the minute our mind goes idle. It's the worst kind of clutter—and it's exactly the chaos we're all so desperately trying to escape.

When's the last time you sat quietly without the impulse to pick up your phone? Have you ever tried to meditate or pray and instead found your mind spinning, moving quickly from one thought to the next? We've been programmed to instinctively seek the next rush of entertainment, productivity, or learning, to find ways to do more with our time. And those constant urges are the very thing that is complicating our lives and preventing us from being able to unplug, slow down, and rest. We're just going through the motions as we rush on to the next thing. Yet at the end of it all, it's those insignificant, daily moments in our lives that truly write our stories. True love, marriage, the dream home, the dream job, babies—those big life events all command attention for a brief time. But there are millions of beautiful everyday moments falling amidst those major milestones that truly define who we are and the lives we lead.

Think back to your childhood. What are the memories that flash most brightly through your mind? I bet they're not about an overly decorated birthday party, an elaborate stack of Christmas presents by the tree, or even your high school graduation, your first date, or your winning goal on the soccer field. I bet most of them are what you'd deem insignificant: a flash of lying on your childhood bed with the windows open and the curtains rustling as a cool spring breeze rushes past your cheeks; or a drive through the mountains, beach-bound, singing at the top of your lungs to your parents' favorite songs. They could be of a warm embrace with your childhood dog, your hands combing through his soft, silky fur; the lovely floral smell emanating from your grandmother's peonies, plucked fresh from the garden; or the aromas wafting off slowly simmering onion and garlic as you stood by the stove, learning your family's secret sauce recipe as your mother smiled on with pride.

There's a reason why those are the memories that stuck. It's because those are the ones that *mattered*.

These are the moments you're after. These are the moments that can provide you with the motivation to pursue the simple, the mundane, the everyday—to seek it out and find the joy in it. Because when you start doing that, every day becomes special.

Every day becomes an intentional one. And if that isn't enough of a reason to seek out the simple, I don't know what is.

GET READY TO LET GO

If you're looking to pare down around your home and find more joy in less, you came to the right place. I'm your girl. But also know that it's going to take more than decluttering and organizing every nook and cranny of your spaces to carve out more room to breathe. Because here's the honest truth: The true joy of simpler living only sustains when you learn to declutter your head and heart, too.

It's not just about letting go of the physical stuff—it's about letting go of all the mental and emotional stuff, too. Moving to a simpler life means letting go of the constant running to-do lists, Pinterest organization boards, and quests for the perfect planner or cleaning routine. Letting go of the expectations you've set for yourself, your home, and your family, and embracing all the ebbs and flows of motherhood with a little bit less of a burden on your shoulders and a little more gratitude in your heart. The process involves taking control of your time and energy and devoting it to the things that matter most to you—not anyone else. Sure, you're going to find plenty of tips here to help make your home simple, functional, and beautiful. But you'll also get a healthy reality check when it comes to infusing simplicity into the rest of your life, too.

Because I promise that will change your life more than any decluttered closet, drawer, or basement.

TUESDAY, MAY 19th

' kiddos! ♥
ut Ⓣ
way

	DUE.
	DOLLARS.

DINNER.
Sausage gnocchi

DON'T FORGET:

TO-DO.

☐ **HEART**
☐ make banana
  muffins

nstall
☐ play legos
☐ Ⓔ art activity
☐ read highlights
☐ Ⓗ rainboots out
☐ PUDDLE JUMPING!

TO DO

HOME
☐ touch up trim
☐ steam playroom
    carpets
☐ call vet
☐ dust
☐ put away
⭐ laundry

CHAPTER 2

A Simpler Schedule

For most of us, motherhood feels like there are just not enough minutes in a day. Between laundry, meals, cleaning, shopping, and raising those kids, our days can quickly morph into one big blur.

But it doesn't have to be that way.

There's a reason why a simpler schedule is the first action item when it comes to a simpler motherhood. Where you spend your time will determine how you spend your days. You can't multitask during every waking minute and expect to reap the benefits of a slower, simpler day. The first step? Take more off your plate.

I know, I know; it's hard to imagine removing any of the essentials of motherhood from your daily to-do list. We all have dishes to clean, laundry to fold, bums to wipe, and boo-boos to kiss. We have fifteen meals and snacks for which to plan, shop, and prepare. We have sticky floors to clean, and crumb-filled carpets to vacuum. But those aren't the most important parts of our days. What's most important? That is up for you to decide. But I'm guessing it'll include enjoying your day with your loved ones. And if you make that your priority—and stop adding on to your to-do list for the sake of getting yet more things done—I think you'll quickly realize how much joy will be added back into your motherhood.

There's a cleaning schedule out there for every personality type under the sun. There are fifteen different planners and apps to help you plot out your days more essentially. And there's a reminder in your phone for almost every single one of those "necessary tasks." But none of that hyper-organization or productivity is going to provide you with the ability to be a happier, calmer mother.

So are you ready to make room for those moments? Let's get started.

REMOVE EVERYTHING, THEN ADD THE BEST BACK IN

I spent years of my life as a mother to little ones attempting to maximize my days; researching all the best methods to accomplish any parenting or home maintenance task required of me; finding the best ways to do it all. And do you know what happened?

I did it all. And it was exhausting.

I'm not proud of the number of times I told a fussy toddler whining to be held, "Hold on a minute, baby. I'm almost finished," or the number of times I'd look at a completely crossed-off to-do list, proud of my accomplishments, and then collapse on the couch, too exhausted to play with my kids, whip up a healthy dinner, or even make conversation with my husband.

Mamas, this "I can do it all" mentality needs to stop. We can do it all—but at a cost. You will without a doubt completely burn yourself out acting on that belief. Your house may be clean and your laundry may be done, but your family will not be getting the best of you.

Let's stop pretending we can get all the things done and still be the best version of ourselves. It's just not possible. And even if it was, is that what you want for your everyday—a checklist to complete? I would rather float through my days prioritizing the most important stuff, and knowing that the rest will all get done in due time. It always does.

Let's stop living in this mentality of *doing* it all and instead shift to a mindset of *being present* for it all. How many nights have you laid in bed reflecting on your day, unable to recall most of what happened? It's amazing how much more meaningful your day becomes when you're actually experiencing the moments that compose it. So how do you make it all simpler?

Start Saying No

In our society today, more usually means better. A large checklist of items to do? You must be productive. More activities for your kids to attend? They're so cultured and well-rounded. More coffee dates, dinner dates, and appointments? You're well-liked and fun to be around.

What if we just said no to it all? I challenge you to remove all of it from your schedule: every single appointment, playdate, activity, and to-do. Remove it all and take a close look. How many of those items are enjoyable? How many of them are getting you to any of your chosen goals? Are you enjoying those coffee dates? Are your kids enjoying all those activities? Do you really need to accomplish every item on your to-do list right now?

My guess is, probably not. Find the ones that speak to your heart. The activities that add to your life; the ones that bring joy and are worthy of your precious time. Hold tight to those and fight to keep them in your days. The rest of it?

Let. It. Go.

Cancel the playdates. Don't sign your child up for another sport. Cross cleaning the baseboards off your to-do list (no one notices, I promise). And spend that freed-up time focusing on what we're about to tackle next.

Start Saying Yes

I know, you're probably thinking, "Didn't you just tell me to say no to everything?" I did. I told you to say no to everything currently taking up your time. My guess is that when you added many of those activities, tasks, and obligations to your schedule, you didn't sit down and ask yourself in an intentional way how they fit into what you wanted for your life. I'd be willing to bet that you didn't stop to wonder if you found joy in those commitments. Many of them were probably added out of obligation, guilt, desire to please, or some other external pressure.

Now that those are gone, I want you to think about what you want this new, simpler, space-and-grace-filled life to look like. What types of moments would you like to include in your every-day? What activities bring you and those close to you joy? What moments make your days exclusively yours? Find what those components are and make room for them.

Maybe it's having enough time in the morning to savor a full cup of hot coffee with your husband; having a few minutes to devote to cracking a book during nap time; or having the actual freedom to stop doing chores and play with your kids down on the floor simply because you can.

Maybe it's something new. You've always wanted to have your own garden...but you've never had the time or mental capacity to research, build, and maintain it. Or you've dreamed of having some free time to devote to something like volunteering at your child's school, photography, or even starting a blog. Whatever it is, prioritize it. What your heart wants is important. Find ways to build that into your schedule however you can. Start saying yes to those "one day" dreams and add them to your days.

Start Questioning It All

Most importantly, don't forget that our life is composed of seasons. We grow and change as individuals, and our days must adapt to that. Stop trying to maintain a flawlessly clean home, perfectly organize your closets, and get home-cooked dinners from scratch on the table when you've got three kids under five to keep alive (trust me, I've been there). Be honest and realistic about the stage of life you're in, and build your schedule accordingly. It may take some time. There might be learning experiences. You may have to go back and clear your schedule out a week, a month, or a year down the line and start all over again.

That's okay. As our lives change, our schedules should reflect that. What does that mean? You must keep putting in the work. You can't just do a one-time reset of your schedule and assume it'll work well for you and your family years down the line. A simpler life is about constant revision, shifting, and most importantly, intentional evaluation. It takes work to match your schedule and your time to your needs, and when you're a mom, your needs and those of your family are going to constantly change and evolve. Be willing to do the same. Be ready to be frustrated; it's going to happen. And when you start feeling like the commitments in your days are no longer serving you, be brave enough to acknowledge it and adjust.

Sometimes, those tweaks may be small and easy. Other times, they might be big and challenging. Be prepared to encounter them all and adapt your days to better serve you. In seasons of chaos, remove more to add some calm and space. In seasons of slowness, try something new—a new dinner recipe, a new hobby, a new route on your morning walk—and savor all the joy that the unknown and new can add to your days.

MAKE A WEEKLY TO-DO LIST

One of the biggest things I see fellow mothers struggle with is keeping up with their to-do lists. I've tried every method, system, and routine under the sun to clean my home, organize my closets, and stay on top of the daily grind. And I failed horribly at all of them. Sure, if you try enough, you'll find a close fit; a rhythm or routine that *almost* works well for you. But I've found that as with most other things in life, it's best to carve out your own path.

For me, that means making a weekly to-do list versus a daily one. I don't have a cleaning schedule; I don't force myself to tackle certain tasks on certain days (unless it's urgent or needed). Most weeks, I assemble a loose to-do list that contains all the necessary action items for the week, and then I make it my goal to get them done as I have the time, energy, and motivation. Sometimes, that means knocking out laundry, cleaning bathrooms, and mopping the floors all on a Monday morning. Other times, that means actually getting a home-cooked dinner on the table and calling it a day. Some weeks it means foregoing all the necessary chores because I've got a sick kid, the toddlers aren't sleeping well, or I just don't feel up to it.

And do you know what I do when that happens? I roll those to-dos over to the next week. Or I delegate them to my husband. Or I just don't get them done. Guess what? Life goes on. I give myself grace. I refocus my attention to what's needed in that moment, and I prioritize my time accordingly. The toilets can wait; my sobbing daughter can't. I remove the pressure of feeling like my day was only successful if I checked items off my list, and I shift my perspective to what truly adds up to a fulfilled motherhood: moments lived, not tasks completed.

I know how hard it can be to "just" be a mom. It can be easy to validate your role to your partner, your friends, and even yourself when you can list the tasks you've completed in a day—when you have something tangible done to show for all the hours you've been at home. But let me tell you, you can't put a value on being there to kiss a pinched finger or help assemble a blanket fort. You may not be able to see all the hours you spent explaining where the sun goes at night, or be able to tangibly justify the hours of patience you mustered dealing with an epic toddler tantrum. But it *matters*. Your kind of work is the most important kind: raising caring, honest, and good human beings to help make this world a better place. The to-dos can wait—trust me. The laundry might pile up, and the toilets might start growing some interesting colors of mold, but those chores will get done eventually. Your day should be planned around your most important work: helping those little humans grow, keeping them happy, and making sure they know they are loved and that they are your most important to-do of the day.

PICK YOUR TOP THREE

I know, I know—things need to get done. Not all the things, all at once, but there are always things that may need to be tackled so that life can continue functioning. Maybe it's shopping for groceries—there's no milk, bread, or eggs in sight, and you need something other than macaroni and cheese to make it through the day. Perhaps it's a load of laundry to avoid running out of clean underwear and having to turn your current pair inside out (yes, I've been there). Or maybe it's finally running the dishwasher or tackling that sink full of dishes so that you've got a clean plate to eat off for breakfast.

Sometimes, there are things that just *need* to be done to keep your home functional. But there's usually only a few "must-do" items. I try to focus on three top priorities each morning. Plug them into your phone, write them on a sticky note, jot them in your planner—whatever they are, those should be your main tasks for the day.

Don't let a glimpse of dusty baseboards or a disorganized playroom sidetrack you and prevent you from tackling your priorities for the day. Three tasks—it's simple enough not to feel overwhelmed, yet it's enough to make you feel like you're at least staying on top of the basics and keeping your home from spiraling into a dirty, disordered mess. A reminder: These tasks aren't about always having your home completely clean or tidy. They're about keeping things in a maintained state so that you're never feeling totally overwhelmed and out of control. Remember: your priority is to enjoy your days and spend time with those little people whenever you're able to.

A lot of people assume that a simple, minimal life is about everything being perfect all the time. But that couldn't be further from the truth. Life is messy! Living in a home with little ones means actually *living* there. A simpler home is one where *you* are uncluttered, too, not just your shelves. It's about freeing up space to focus on actually interacting with and listening to your kids, taking a walk with the dog, or cooking a dinner from scratch. It's about being present in the here and now and enjoying your life exactly how it is in this moment, imperfect as it may be. It's about getting out of the "what's next" mentality and being intentional about how you spend your time. And I promise, your home will be clean, things will get done, and life will run perhaps even a little bit smoother without the burden of an overwhelming list of tasks to tackle every single day.

BALANCE HOME AND HEART

One of my favorite concepts that I've borrowed from a dear friend is the separation of Home and Heart when it comes to my daily tasks.

Every day, when I write out my to-do lists and examine my calendar, I make sure to balance out tasks that fulfill needs within my home and within my heart. This usually means three "home" tasks and three "heart" tasks each day.

My home list is composed of some pretty mundane, familiar to-dos: Call the bank. Pull weeds in the garden. Clean the bathrooms. Mop the floors. It's made up of all the basics that need to be accomplished to maintain our home and keep our family functioning.

My heart list is my favorite. It's composed of the tasks that will bring joy to my heart and to the hearts of my loved ones, things like setting up a new craft for the kids, going on a walk as a family around the neighborhood, or sending my husband a thank-you text for unloading the dishwasher and getting up early with the baby. Heart list tasks also can include self-care items like painting my chipped toenails or being able to take a hot shower in peace—or heck, just using the bathroom with the door locked! (Are anyone else's kids still struggling to understand what privacy means?) Whatever it is, I make sure those tasks occupy my days as well. After all, I'd dare say they're a bit more important than a clean toilet or a weeded garden bed.

By making sure I have both types of tasks on my to-do list, it refocuses my time and energy and allocates it more appropriately. We're all guilty of that "Just one more minute—I've got to finish this!" line. And making sure I've got my priorities evenly balanced between home tasks and time with my kids and husband (as well as myself!) ensures I find a way to incorporate the best things in my life almost every single day.

After all, that's what being at home with your kids is about, right? It's not about being home to have everything perfectly clean and organized, or cooking elaborate, healthy meals from scratch. You are home with your children to do life with them, to raise them, teach them, grow with them—to *be with them.* Don't spend the majority of your days maintaining a home. Spend it with those little pieces of your heart. They won't be little forever, and they definitely need you more than those dusty cabinets do.

FACE IT: THINGS CHANGE

This may perhaps be the most important component of building a simpler schedule, because if there's one thing we know about life—and motherhood, specifically—it's that just when you feel as if you've mastered something, it changes.

Bummer, right? I know. You were hoping this chapter held a magical, life-changing solution that you'd never found to simplify your days and hours and make them efficient and enjoyable—indefinitely. But alas, it does not. And honestly, I'm fairly certain that type of solution doesn't exist. I should know; I spent years attempting to fit myself into so many different cleaning schedules, list-making and planner approaches, and even daily rhythms that just didn't work for me and my children. I may have gotten things done, but it wasn't simple, and it sure wasn't enjoyable.

It's frustrating always having to adapt, change, and start anew again. And doing this with your time can be especially frustrating. But life changes. We change. It *all* changes. That's life. And it's how you flex with those changes as life unfolds that will ultimately

determine whether you operate on a flowing, simpler schedule...
or feel like banging your head against a wall.

Learn to be more adaptable. As you try things, you may find
some concepts just don't work well for you and your home, or
that others work extremely well. If there's one thing I've learned
about simplifying, it's that there's no one-size-fits-all approach.
We're all so different; our lives are different, our personalities
are different, and our children and their needs are different.
Find methods and concepts that work well for you, and don't feel
guilty about discarding the rest. Don't try to force yourself into
a schedule or routine that just isn't serving you. Borrow from
different approaches: Take the most valuable components and
create your own system. Create your own schedule. Create your
own life. Isn't that the beauty of it all? We're not designing a life or
living our days for anyone other than ourselves and the people
closest to us. And once our schedule aligns with our values, our
life becomes more authentically ours.

Most importantly, don't be afraid of change. Don't let the concept
of the unknown or the unfamiliar scare you. Find a new reality for
yourself and pursue it fearlessly. Discomfort is often a necessity
for impactful, life-altering change. Embrace it, and give yourself
time to adjust. It's going to feel weird when you free up space
and allow your mind to change accordingly. Your family and
friends are going to notice and make comments that may be
uncomfortable to address. Your kids may not know what to do
with all that free time they now have in their days. Give yourself
and your loved ones time to adjust to the change. Anything good
in life requires effort and persistence, and when your head, heart,
and home adjust accordingly, you'll be eternally grateful you let
yourself sit with that discomfort while the change rolls in.

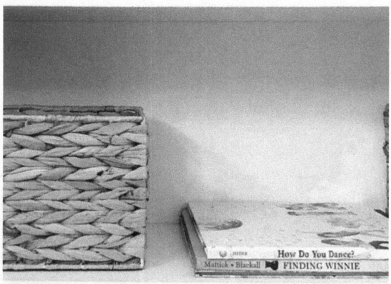

CHAPTER 3

Simpler Spaces

I bet I know why you picked up this book. And I'm probably about to burst your bubble.

I know this because I can't count how many decluttering, minimalism, and home organization books I've consumed, hoping to find the solution that would help me clear the clutter and have a home that felt organized, simplified, and orderly for the rest of time. But the reality is this: As with everything else in life, simpler living is a journey, not a destination.

So if you're just here for practical tips to help you create perfectly organized linen closets, pantries, and wardrobes—go ahead and put this book down. Like, right now.

Are you still here?

Good. You're my people. Because simpler spaces are a constant, evolving, imperfect thing—but the world will lead you to believe otherwise. Just switch on the TV or scroll through social media: show after show and feed after feed of before-and-after perfection. Clutter-filled, outdated, stress-inducing spaces are magically transformed into perfectly staged, curated homes right before your eyes.

It's downright addictive. I've been there. And it gives us all the hope in the world that we, too, can buy a gallon of paint, grab a handful of trash bags, and make our home a perfect haven. Sure, that's possible. But guess what?

It's all temporary. All of it. Because your home is meant to be lived in. And lived in, it is. Regardless of the systems you have in place, the mountains of items you purge, or the number of organizational bins you purchase, nothing will ever be perfectly in place all the time.

But that doesn't mean you can't make your home the best it can be. And how do you do that, exactly?

LEARN TO LOVE WHAT YOU'VE GOT

Learning to embrace your current reality is perhaps the biggest hurdle to overcome when your goal is getting to a simpler space. We're bombarded with the constant need to upgrade, improve, and chase after bigger and better things. And it's easy to get sucked in by the excitement of purging your spaces and going out to buy all the new things to fill them because we're constantly being sold the message that new things will make us happy.

Does new stuff make me happy? Absolutely. But it's a fleeting happiness. Do you know what creates a more permanent, sustainable happiness? Pride. Contentment. What really makes me happy is accepting and embracing what I've got right here, right now, and making it work in the best ways I can.

This goes for far more than your home's aesthetic—it translates into the way you view yourself, your children, your partner, your family. It's a contagious perspective in the very best way. And the sooner you learn to find this type of internal, self-driven happiness with the things you own, the sooner it'll flood the rest of your life with the same glorious joy.

But let's get back to your home. Look around the room you're currently sitting in. I bet your mind immediately goes to all the things you don't love about that space: the clutter spilling out of the TV cabinet, the unorganized toys littering the floor, the ugly paint color on the walls, the outdated piece of furniture that you use daily but wish you could upgrade to a trendy, new piece. Guess what? It's all fixable, without throwing out a single thing or spending a dime. (Although once we're done, you may want to wisely do both.) Because simpler living or minimalism—whatever you want to call it—is a lifestyle, not an aesthetic.

Minimalism isn't about having the least amount of stuff. It's about owning and consuming only the things you *love* and *use*. That's why simpler living looks different for everyone. There's no magic number of things that will get you to your goal. No rules; no limits; and most importantly, no "end point" or "destination." Because it's a lifelong journey; a conscious lifestyle. It's stepping off the mindless path of consumption that most of the world is following and blazing your own path to less with intention and purpose.

So whether you've finally made this the year you begin to pursue a life of less or you're already well on your way, remember this: You make the rules. You get to decide what people and things fill your life, your home, your heart, and your head. Choose wisely. Keep those that matter—and let the rest go. The minute you embrace the things in your home and value them for what they are and how they serve you, you'll be in a better position to create a space that sparks joy, makes your day-to-day easier, and allows you to spend less time focusing on your stuff and a lot more time focusing on your people.

The Valuable Things

You simply can't declutter or materially simplify your home and expect lasting change if you don't take the time to figure out what truly holds value to you. I've seen it time and time again—heck, I've lived it many times over. Getting rid of stuff without doing the emotional heavy lifting that comes with identifying what matters to you most simply creates a temporary space in your home that will eventually be refilled with more things.

Why? Because if we don't start assessing the value in items, we continue to seek joy by purchasing and amassing things that clearly don't do that. And then, weeks, months, or years later, we're stuck making those decisions when our closets, attics, or storage units are again filled to the brim. And when we go to get rid of those items (most often unused or lightly used), we struggle to let go after spending money on them.

Valuable things are those items that are functional, provide you with increased productivity, and help make your life easier. And there are a lot of these essentials in all of our homes, especially when our children are at different ages and stages of life. Motherhood requires a *lot* of stuff—I get it.

But when we're talking about value, I'm talking about the stuff that you actually use, not the items that cost you an arm and a leg to purchase yet sit in the basement gathering dust (hey treadmill, I'm talking to you). An item may be quite expensive, but if it's just in your way and not being used (and could be extremely useful to someone else), it needs to go.

I know, I know; you spent good money on those things. You thought you would use them. Or you might still believe you'll possibly use them one day. Guess what? You're not throwing away your money by donating them or passing them along to a friend or family member. The money was gone a long time ago. You wasted the money when you purchased that item, not when you decided it no longer served you. You're simply finding a new home for that item where it will be put to good use.

This includes all those just-in-case items cluttering up your garages, basements, closets, and storage units. I have an easy rule for those items: If you haven't found a use for them in the past year, you most likely won't be using them in the next one. Donate it, sell it, or find a new home for it—one where it will be doing more than serving as a placeholder and gathering dust.

And while we're talking "valuable," please remember: we all value different things. There's no one-size-fits-all, blanket definition for what value means to you. In fact, what you value most in your home may be very different from what your children or your partner value. That is completely normal and totally okay. Why? Because your home is a shared space. Make sure to recognize that and value things accordingly. It's not worth sacrificing an item someone you love values for the sake of a less cluttered home that aligns with your vision. Your loved ones will always matter more than perfecting your space—or your things. This may mean that certain areas of your home—your partner's closet, your child's playroom—don't look like you expect or want them to. But it's important to respect their boundaries and their values, because what matters most should be what they love, not how similar or aligned each room and space in your home are.

Value is simply the quality of a thing that helps you operate more easily on a day-to-day basis. It's not a monetary or sentimental thing, it's simply functional: What items in your home make motherhood easier? What items help simplify your systems, routines, and daily life? Hold onto those items, and get ready to discard the rest. With one exception...

The Beautiful Things

There are so many beautiful things in this life, and they're meant to be enjoyed. A simpler life isn't about eliminating anything that isn't functional, it's about eliminating the excess so that you have more space in your home, your life, and your schedule to *enjoy* all the beautiful things. Because those are the very best kind.

Maybe it's that coffee mug your six-year-old made in art class—lumpy, bumpy, and covered in paint splatters, but crafted with love. You may smirk with laughter at its imperfections, but the love that went into creating that mug makes it beautiful to you. Maybe it's a fresh vase of peonies from your weekly trip to the grocery store—oozing the most pervasively beautiful scent, one that reminds you of summers in your grandmother's garden. Perhaps it's that framed family photo, that extra cozy knit throw blanket, or even that worn, cozy, slipcovered armchair in the corner of your living room. Whatever it is, *hold onto it for dear life*. That beauty is intangible, and it provides more joy in your life than you may realize.

It may not provide a ton of function. It may not serve any purpose other than to make you smile every time you catch a glimpse of it in your home. But that feeling of joy is *invaluable*. Don't miss out on peppering your home with items that look and feel beautiful to you. They may hold more space in your heart than you consciously know, and the payout they contribute to all the joys of a simpler life is what you're going for. After all, what's the purpose of curating a simpler home if there's nothing within those walls to appreciate?

While we're talking about beauty, it's important to remember that beauty is such a subjective thing—it's different for every person. And it spans far more than just stuff. We're talking experiences, feelings, and moods, too. We're talking about the candle that fills your home with the most glorious citrus scents; that ugly, tattered family quilt that's perfectly broken in, softer than life itself, and wraps you in memories each time you're chilly; that wooden bench out under your favorite backyard shade tree, grey with age, but the perfect respite on a hot summer day. They may not be beautiful in the obvious sense, and they may take up space in your home, but they also offer up a sensory experience that adds immeasurable amounts of happiness to your days.

And it's never, *ever* clutter if it makes you happy.

EMBRACE YOUR SEASON

Speaking of a home you enjoy, let me remind you that minimalism and simpler living are about appreciating what is beautiful to you and what works for the season of life that you're currently in. It's not just a sparsely furnished room with clean lines and modern furniture, void of life. Living simply doesn't have to mean living in an all-white box (although I personally do love heavy doses of white in my home décor) or cold, bare walls and rooms. When you're raising children and growing a family, simple living is going to look very different. That's not to say that you can't paint your entire home white and raise happy children; it's just that sometimes, you must adjust your expectations for what a simple home will look and feel like to you in this stage of your life.

As our family has learned to simplify our budget and our stuff, I've learned to let go of the perfect image I'd painted in my mind of the way a simple home should look. I'd love to furnish our home with less-but-better furniture, but that just isn't practical or realistic. Instead, we invest in a lot of hand-me-downs and inexpensive-but-simple DIY projects and finishes that can last us through this stage of life with four little ones. And more importantly, I do my very best to embrace the fact that in this season of motherhood, imperfect is the name of the game.

Our home is old, as are many of our furnishings. But it's all well-loved and well-worn, and most importantly, it functions for us as a young family. It may be used, chipped, or slightly wobbly, but all those things still bring me immense joy because I've embraced them and their presence in my home and stopped expecting my home to look like a photo in a magazine. Instead, I focus on caring for what I'm grateful to have *right now*, rather than planning for what I *could* have down the line.

FIND THE BEAUTY IN IMPERFECTION

You can be a minimalist *and* a mom.

Let me repeat that. Minimalism and motherhood aren't two mutually exclusive lifestyles. I know, I know—it sure is easier to have more space in your home when you don't have little humans running around and cluttering it up. But that doesn't mean it's not possible. It's very possible *if* you adjust your expectations.

Don't put off simplifying your home until your kids grow up. Please, please know that it doesn't have to be an all-or-nothing process. I think that's what stops most of us from chasing after the goals we want for ourselves in every aspect of our lives, whether it's losing ten pounds, finding time to pursue a hobby, or making the effort to carve out a new habit. There will never be a perfect time to start, and if you keep putting it off, you'll be exactly where you are right now (or worse), but with days, weeks, or years lost in waiting for the moment to change your life.

You didn't get to where you are right now overnight. It's a culmination of days, weeks, and years of decisions and actions. And you can expect the same if you're pursuing a life of less, whether you have kids or not. Sure, it'll look different. It may take longer. You may feel that if you can't do it perfectly, why even do it at all? Why? Because progress is still progress, however big or small, and because simpler living is about creating a life that feels and looks simpler to *you* and no one else. Don't let the expectations of what a simpler, more minimal home looks and feels like to other people in different stages of their lives affect whether you make the decision to go for it, either.

Listen, I get it, more than you probably know. In fact, as I sit here right now, perched in a cozy armchair in our living room, I gaze around at the "clutter": the old coffee table I scored for cheap at a yard sale and refinished in the driveway the first year we were married, littered with toys, with its painted legs chipped from years of use. The baby swing and pack-and-play that dominate the room, forcing us to push our furniture closer together in a less-than-ideal spacing to allow for life with a three-month-old. It's far from the image I have in my mind of a perfect living room.

But it's *home*. It's lived in. And at this stage of our lives, it's as simplified and decluttered as it can be. For now, it's what will work for our family as we prioritize functionality while raising four kids six and under. Don't get me wrong—it's still hard. I still feel pangs of jealousy when I scroll through feeds of beautifully styled new builds, or even stylishly decorated old homes, void of all the clutter that comes with young children. But it stops there. Because it's only temporary. It's clutter, sure—but it's the *best* kind of clutter.

You'll get new furniture someday. All the baby things will be packed up and stored in the basement or sold to a friend in just a few short months. That clutter will all be gone in a few short years—it won't last forever. You can fight an uphill battle, or you can learn to make peace with a certain level of imperfection in your space. Make that choice to embrace a little chaos, and your definition of what a simpler life looks like with children will instantly change for the better.

DECLUTTERING 101: THE PREP WORK

So hopefully, by now, you're understanding the importance of having the right mindset and setting up some deeper patterns of thinking and behaving so you can make some lasting changes to your home. You're ready to get rid of the extra stuff—I get it. And you're desperately hoping I'm about to provide you with some super helpful decluttering advice for streamlining your stuff. Hang in there, because that's coming up in later chapters.

But for now, we need to focus on the big picture: some elementary yet ever-so-important concepts that are essential before we begin the simplifying process. Bear with me—I know you're ready for all the nitty-gritty details, but these concepts are important to help you achieve lasting space in your home, your head, and your heart without burning out.

A Drawer at a Time

It's easy to get a sudden, impulsive urge to purge your stuff and immediately want to do it all. I totally understand that, because I get those impulses all the time. If you're like me, you want to tackle the biggest project first—you know, that overflowing basement storage room or the completely cluttered garage; or that filled-to-the-brim master closet holding more clothing than you know what to do with. Sounds like a good idea, right?

Wrong. Because simplifying your home takes time and energy— two things that most moms don't have in vast quantities. Let's start small and tackle things in a more practical way: a drawer and a room at a time.

I know it's underwhelming and probably disappointing to hear that. You want to make a major impact. You want your home to instantly feel more spacious, less cluttered, and tidier. But things didn't pile up overnight, and you won't be able to instantly remove them in one day. By tackling one large project, you're setting yourself up for failure. It's the equivalent of diving into the deep end when you're just learning to swim. Sure, you might be able to keep yourself afloat, but you're going to end up exhausted—without much to show for it.

Instead, we're going to tackle things in a more manageable and sustainable way. As you approach each space in your room, remind yourself that you're not trying to overhaul your entire space but instead setting up a motivating, snowball-type effect that will help you continue to work at it in smaller pieces. Little projects not only make a huge difference in the way your day-to-day feels, but seeing a small space completely transformed in a short amount of time is incredibly addictive. I mean, have you ever impulsively tackled that kitchen junk drawer when you just couldn't take it anymore? It might have just been one small drawer, but the emotional and mental clutter that dissipates when that tiny space is organized and streamlined opens up a world of calm and a sense of productivity. That's the feeling we're going for when we tackle each space in our home.

Just promise me this: Don't get ahead of yourself. If you tackle one small drawer, shelf, or storage basket and feel motivated to move on to another, go for it. But it's far easier to make the decision to add another small project into your agenda than it is to tackle some large, massive room and quickly realize you don't have the time (or energy) to finish it.

Work smarter, not harder. It's more productive, every time.

Streamline the Smart Way

While we're discussing the smartest way to attack your clutter, let's talk strategy. Where do I start? It's a question I'm constantly asked. And I provide the exact same answer every single time: It depends.

It depends on what's tripping you up the most in your day-to-day. I always suggest you identify the biggest pain points in your home whenever you're trying to declutter and simplify, for two very good reasons: Clearing them up makes an instant impact, and they don't add more work to an already-busy schedule.

Those spaces are going to be different for everyone. Maybe your closet is a nightmare and you spend every morning taking twenty minutes just to root through all the clothing to find your favorite black top, buried in the mess of things you never wear. Maybe it's your kitchen cabinets, crammed so full of bowls, plates, and cups that you can barely close the door. Or perhaps it's that Tupperware drawer overflowing with containers and tops, none of which seem to fit together. Maybe it's your laundry room—so full of clothing piles that you can't tell the clean from the dirty; or the playroom shelves, stuffed with bins of disorganized toys, many broken or unused. Or it could be the bathroom linen closet, spilling expired medications each time you reach for a clean towel. Whatever space it is that provides you with a constant headache and slows you down the most on a daily basis, identify it. That's where you'll begin.

Embrace Decluttering Purgatory

Quite possibly one of the biggest hang-ups on the way to releasing clutter is the hesitation to let things go. And I get it. You spent your hard-earned money on these items. You had good intentions of using them. You think perhaps they will be things you'll need at some point. Or maybe that was a white elephant gift, or perhaps a reminder of the past. Maybe it holds some great sentimental value to you.

Here's the thing: The money was spent when you bought the item, not when you decided to let it go. And those good intentions were noble, but circumstances or seasons have changed, and that item no longer serves you. And that gift or that sentimental item? The experience or memory attached to that item is what holds the most value. It's not going anywhere, even if you get rid of it.

So get ready to let a lot of it go.

But before your anxiety spikes at the thought of letting go of all these things, know that you're in control. You're the best person to evaluate the usefulness and the meaning of your items, as well as whether there is a need to retain them. I'm not here to tell you to get rid of every item you're not using daily, or to purge what's providing you joy, but I'm going to challenge you to *really look* at how each thing in your home serves you. Remember: It's just stuff. You can't take it with you when you go. And you'll be leaving it all behind for your loved ones to deal with. If it's not serving you in your daily endeavors or bringing you intense joy, it's time to consider letting it leave your home. After all, each pocket of space you open up in your house allows you the opportunity to bring in experiences or things that will add to your life.

To further alleviate that stress and anxiety, let me share what is possibly my favorite strategy when it comes to a simpler home: decluttering purgatory. It's a simple concept, but it's so, *so* effective—and you may unknowingly be doing this already. But it's made my decluttering journey so much simpler and more productive that I'd be remiss if I didn't share it with you.

My emotional ties to my things were one of the biggest hurdles I faced when trying to simplify my home. I've always loved a good purging spree, and I was often ruthless with getting rid of items in my home that I was certain I didn't use or love anymore. But I constantly hesitated on that "maybe" pile, which was often my largest category. You know what I'm talking about: all those items that you just couldn't definitively throw into the donation pile during all your previous decluttering attempts, so you held onto them for "later," when you'd have more time; when you would know for certain that you didn't need it.

Except later never happened. Because with each purge, you kept pushing it off for next time—until now. Meet decluttering purgatory: your new best friend. It'll change the way you view decluttering and remove the emotional, time-sucking decisions from your efforts.

Here's how it works: Every item you're unsure about eliminating from your home—regardless of the reason—goes into a box or bin and is then stored out of sight for a period of time. You pick the place: your storage room, your basement, your garage, the back of your closet. You pick the time: a week, a month, or a year from now. You put all those "maybe" items into the box or bins, and you store it away. And most likely, you forget about it.

The items aren't leaving your home—they're not being sold or donated. They're just being put to the test to see whether you *truly* need them. And they're right there in your basement, storage room, or closet, if you utilize this technique. You can easily go get an item and return it to its proper place, because if you consciously thought of the item and had a need for it, it deserves to stay. But if within that week, month, or year, they're still in the box...it's pretty clear that you didn't have a true need or use for those things.

Decluttering purgatory removes the anxiety around letting go of things you think will be useful or meaningful to you at a later time. This process loosens the emotional ties we have to our things and shows you what truly matters and is needed in your life. I've been using this concept for years, and do you want to know how many things I've gone and removed from my boxes?

One. One item. And that was only due to an earnest request for an old toy from my daughter. Also, that toy went right back into the box after a few short weeks (and was later donated).

Sometimes, we all just need validation that we don't truly love all the things or need them to be happy.

Your House Is Not a Storage Space

You're ready to make your house a home. You want to remove the excess and keep only the things you love and use in your daily spaces. That basement or that storage closet is meant to hold all the extra, right?

Nope. We live in a society that constantly sells us the idea that stuff makes us important. We therefore amass it all—anything we feel makes life easier or that makes us feel more important; anything that tells the world that we matter or that makes us feel like a part of the bigger whole. And when those things start piling up in our main living spaces, well, we just buy a bigger house. With a bigger closet. And a bigger basement. Or even better, we just conveniently rent a monthly storage unit, where we can hold onto that stuff until we have the room—or the need—for it.

Sounds ridiculous when you break it down, right?

Whether you live in a one-bedroom apartment or a 5,000 square foot home, a simpler life is possible. You don't need to *buy* more space—you need to *make* more space. And that's easily done, regardless of how much stuff you own or how many square feet you've got to work with. I know the urge is to hold on to the items we think we'll use or need "one day," but let me remind you that your house is a home, not a storage facility. The walls you live within, where you spend your days, should hold items that serve you or bring you joy, and very little more.

And while we're talking about storage spaces in your home, let me remind you that holding on to things "just in case" is a waste of your space and time. Sure, you may have the physical room to store those items. But why? I know it's convenient to have items on hand "just in case," but is that convenience worth the cost of storing, organizing and maintaining those items while they're sitting there, waiting to maybe, possibly be used in the near future? That's something you'll have to figure out on your own—we all have different expectations for the level of minimalism we'd like in our home. And that's the beauty of simple living: There's no one-size-fits-all formula for the number of items a minimal home ought to hold. It depends on so many different factors—where you live, how many children you have, what you value. The important takeaway is this: Hold on to only those items that bring value to your life, your family, and your home—and let go of everything else.

How Valuable is Your Time?

Now, once we've decided we're parting with things that no longer hold value to us, there are several ways to get rid of them. The three most common are trash, donation, or sale. All three avenues have their place, depending on the item. Whenever possible, I aim to do my part to prevent items from going to the landfill by donating or selling them. There will always be broken or unusable things that will end up in the trash. But ideally, most of your items will find a new home, whether they're passed on to someone else for a second life or sold.

Let me remind you that your time is valuable. If you're here seeking a simpler lifestyle for yourself and your family, it bears mentioning. Time is a precious commodity, and having more of it is one of the biggest draws of simpler living. With less stuff in your home, your head, and your heart, there's so much more space to think more clearly, feel more in tune, and do what you want with your life. Remind yourself of this as you're decluttering your home. Selling items and recouping some of their sunken cost is helpful, but often, the time and effort required to do so are simply not worth it compared to the ability to immediately clear a space by donating those items in a simple drop-off or pickup.

Some items are definitely worth selling, especially if they're in good shape or are seen as valuable by a large pool of potential buyers. But just remember, the ultimate goal of simpler living is to have more time to focus on what truly matters. Is making a few bucks on a few minutes or hours of work worth it to you? That's for you to decide.

I also like to consider the emotional benefits of donating versus selling. I am very aware that chasing a more minimal lifestyle is a true privilege—one that not all of us are given. I know that there are plenty of people in this world who are not fortunate enough to have a problem with excess possessions. And that's often the reminder I need to let go of the investment I've made in items that don't currently serve me, allowing me to instead pass along those items to someone who may have a real need for them—someone who'll get much more value from them than they possess sitting unused on a shelf in my basement storage room. Try it. I promise you, any hesitation you may feel to let go of that stuff frequently disappears the moment you change your perspective and remember that there's a person on the receiving end who'll most likely feel extremely grateful to be the recipient of your unused or unneeded goods.

Create a Donation Drop Zone

Hopefully by now I've hammered home the point that decluttering isn't a one-and-done project. A simpler life, like any other lifestyle, requires constant maintenance. You can't go into a room armed with boxes and trash bags, clear out the excess, and assume the work is done. The reality of life is that even as a minimalist, you'll still be a consumer; a more intentional consumer, sure—but a consumer nonetheless. Living still causes us to need things, make purchases, and bring new stuff into our homes. It's going to happen, especially with children, as the seasons of motherhood change and our children grow. As humans, we all require different things in different seasons of life. So, rather than setting ourselves up for failure by trying to eliminate our intake of goods, let's instead focus on setting up an easier system to deal with those items as we move through life and our needs change.

My favorite way to do this? Save the shipping boxes or shopping bags you receive with the items you buy, and use them for items you'll be parting with. It's such a natural, easy way to balance the influx and outflow of things in your home. One item in, one item out—you may have heard of that concept before. But often, we have periods in our lives when we require more things, as well as periods where we let many items go. Think of the first year of life with a baby. It's necessary to acquire so many things—baby swings, baby clothes, baby bottles, baby toys. They all come into our home around the same time, and they all go out quickly after their purpose is served. It's impractical to expect our lives to function with exactly the same number of possessions for all seasons. Some phases require more, others less. But the easiest way I've found to keep that balance is to hold onto all those bags and boxes and fill them as items require an exit.

Those boxes or bags can be kept wherever you're most likely to be reminded to review your need for items. For me, I keep them in our laundry room, as I often end up washing clothing that no longer serves me before I donate it. When it comes out of the dryer, I simply fold it and toss it in the box or bin. No more effort is needed. I don't have to think about it again until that box or bag is full, and then I simply throw it in my trunk and drop it off at the donation center. It's a system that requires minimal thinking, and more importantly, it encourages a continuous cycle of evaluation and editing and makes it so simple when you've got an item that needs to leave your home. Simply add it to the box and move on with your life.

The Minimalism Learning Curve

Last but not least, let me remind you that simpler living isn't a competition. It's not about who has the least stuff. Minimizing your home is important, but it's easy to go too far. And if you take the concept of minimalism too literally, know that there's always an opportunity to turn it back around.

I know this because I lived it. For years, we decluttered. We min-imized. We saved. We budgeted. We stopped trying to keep up with the Joneses. We freed ourselves from that ever-vicious cycle of consumerism. And it felt good. *Really* good.

But still, something was missing. Rather, some *things* were missing.

About a year ago, I realized we'd edited our lives a little too much. We'd tipped the scales a little too far in the other direction. We had peaceful, blank walls, half-empty cabinets, bare countertops, and plenty of breathing room in our bank account. But in the quest for less, we had ruthlessly eliminated some of the things that had brought us the most joy.

Going forward, I decided to do some careful addition. I added our favorite photos to the walls. I added better coffee to our mornings. I added weekly flowers to our grocery list. I added extra money for our favorite takeout into our budget. And by doing that with intention, I carefully added so much life back into our days.

I think we often fail to realize that the desire for less can be just as addictive as the desire for more. The journey to a simpler life is just as much about identifying and holding onto the things that bring you happiness as it is about removing the things that don't. Don't get so carried away with discarding all the clutter that you forget to value what truly brings you joy.

And if you do? Find the courage to reclaim it...one beautiful thing at a time.

CHAPTER 4

Simpler Spending

Money sure is a difficult thing to talk about. But it's important one when you're aiming for making everything in your life a little simpler. Why? Because it's so closely intertwined with a minimal life. Many people chasing after a simpler lifestyle are also hoping to learn how to get rid of their things, stop spending so much money on them, and pay off debts from years of mindless spending. I know I hoped for that. I think it's very rare to find someone who's spending or consuming in excess yet also following a budget. The need for consumption and the urge to spend more money than you should usually go hand-in-hand, and for good reason! When you're overspending, you're most likely making purchases out of impulse or emotionality—two states of being that often don't give a crap what your budget is.

Listen, I know you probably didn't pick up this book to have a writer tell you how to run your finances. But money dictates so much in our lives, from the way we furnish our homes to the way we spend our time. I'm no money expert by any stretch of the imagination. But I am a mom who found herself in way too much unnecessary debt and successfully found a way out of it—without some drastic program, book, or expensive financial advisor. Living simply allows you to focus on the things that matter; to prioritize where your time and energy are going, but just as importantly, your money. Because your time and your energy *are* money. They are two of the most valuable currencies by which we all operate on daily. Let's dive into how to make some small, simple changes to the way we manage our money and how we prioritize where it's going so we can sustain the lifestyles we want to live.

And that all begins with a budget. I get it; budgets aren't sexy—or fun. But they also don't have to be restrictive. In fact, budgets often do the opposite. By telling your money where to go, you take control. You have the power, and with that power comes a ton of freedom. And the first steps to taking control of your finances are the same as taking control of your things: figuring out what matters to you, examining your habits, and finding the joy in less.

WHERE'S THE MONEY GOING?

The first step to figuring out how to take control of your finances is to look to your past spending habits. Where is the money going? What are you spending money on? We're not here to make any instant changes (again, do you sense an overriding theme here?) but rather to simply gather all the information, evaluate our current situation, and develop a plan to create lasting change moving forward. Boring, I know, but let me tell you, it works.

When seeking to simplify your spending, I suggest finding a free budgeting tool and linking all of your checking and savings accounts, credit cards, and investments so that you're able to see each transaction you've made. By examining these purchases and categorizing them, you'll quickly get a picture of where you're putting your money. It's not fun—and it's definitely eye-opening—but it is critical to do this. Again, we're not here to find fault in our prior mistakes, nor to throw everything out the window and start fresh. We're here to examine our habits and create better ones that will set us up for a simpler future—and hopefully, a lot less debt.

Finding the Value

When it comes to money, what matters most? What brings you joy? What experiences or things are your priority? Without figuring this out, your money will be spent on anything that enters the picture and appeals to you. It's essential to sit down and take the time to evaluate what you want for your life—both tangible and experiential—and to manage your finances with a clear outlook on what you're looking to accumulate.

The easiest way to do this is to make a list of what your life goals look like. Want to save up for a down payment on a house, or have enough money to take the family on a summer vacation every year? Maybe it's saving enough for your kids' college education or your retirement fund. Perhaps it's having enough fun money to afford a babysitter and a nice night out. Or maybe it's just saving up as much as possible to pay down your existing debt, even if it means tightening the purse strings and finding ways to cut areas of your budget. Whatever it may be, thinking through where your priorities lie is essential. You need to identify what tangible items or experiences are a priority for you, and then make sure you're creating a budget that aligns with those values.

CREATING A BUDGET

As I mentioned before, examining where your money is going is crucial to beginning to create a budget. Once you've looked at your spending and identified the important, necessary expenses, let's round them up into categories. You don't need an expensive app or budgeting software to do this. There are tons of free apps, and often simply using a pen and paper to create your budget is equally as easy and effective.

As someone who prefers simplicity, the process of creating a budget is no exception. I find forming general categories rather than creating many smaller, more specific categories is the key to an easier, less stressful budget. Here are the essential categories I'd suggest using:

- Mortgage/Rent (including monthly taxes and/or home/ renter's insurance)
- Health Insurance and Medications, as well as other general healthcare costs (including copay contributions and premiums)
- Auto Payments (if applicable)
- Student Loan Payments (if applicable)
- Utilities (electric, water/sewer, phone, trash, internet, television)
- Food (groceries and restaurant meals, and I include home supplies and toiletries here)
- Gas
- Clothing
- Donations
- Education Expenses (tuition, school costs, babysitter and/ or daycare costs)
- Sinking Funds (auto insurance, auto maintenance, gifts, haircuts, entertainment, vacation costs, home furnishings, home improvement and maintenance costs, veterinary costs, periodic medical expenses, and contributions to 401K, IRA, and/or other savings)

Sinking Funds

What is a sinking fund, you may ask? Sinking funds are quite possibly the most amazing way I've found to prevent myself from finding mindless ways to spend the extra money left over after budgeting for the essentials each month. For those of you who are lost right now, a sinking fund is simply an allotment of money for planned purchases that may not occur monthly or may occur at various random times during the year. Think of things like your Christmas spending, or gifts for birthdays. This also includes things like your annual car registration renewal, your car or home insurance, or even a DIY home renovation project you'd like to tackle. They're all expenses that are considered necessary but could quickly derail your budget if you don't account for them.

To add a sinking fund into your monthly budget, all you need to do is write down a list of all these expenses, then estimate what your total spending would be for each. Then divide by twelve to come up with the amount you'll need to contribute each month. It removes the stress when these events or expenses come up, and it gives you more control over your unexpected costs. It also gives you a clearer indication of what your true spending looks like and prevents you from breaking your budget with costs that are unaccounted for each month. Bonus points? If you end up overestimating your sinking fund—which we often do—you end up with a little bonus cash at the end of the year. Either roll it over to start off the year on an even better foot, or use it to treat yourself to something that truly makes you happy. A win-win either way, if you ask me.

Examine Your Spending

Take a look at your past spending and make a good estimate of your spending each month in these categories. Be honest with yourself, and whenever possible, set a realistic amount for each monthly budget category.

Now add those categories up and subtract them from your net income (your gross income minus pre-tax contributions like your 401K, health plan, and other types of insurance). If they add up to more than your net income, you know you've got to go back and rework the budget. Keep doing this until you're left with zero, or even better, with money left over. If you can't get that number to zero by adjusting your budget categories, you're getting a wake-up call: it's time to find a way to increase your income.

Remember, we're looking to do more than spend all the money we're bringing in every month. That extra money will be going toward your savings goals, such as an emergency fund, or paying off debt. These are equally important and worthwhile expenses if you want to get to a simpler, more secure financial situation, so make sure to find ways to contribute funds to these endeavors, however little they may be. Every small contribution adds up.

These budget categories are so critical to taking control of your lifestyle and making things simpler. Budgeting a specific monthly amount for food lets you determine what you can afford to spend on your grocery trips, helps you plan meals that keep you on track, and reminds you to shop more frugally. If I've got a week left in the month and I've hit my monthly max on my food spending, you better believe we're eating leftovers and using what we have on hand to make meals. Deciding on a number for that gas budget category tells me whether we can take that end-of-the-month trip to the zoo or if it's smarter to walk down the street to the park. Having made an intentional decision about spending on my own clothing reminds me that I don't need to buy that tank top (even if it's on sale) and that I've got plenty of ones I love already hanging in my closet, ready to wear and without any additional cost.

See where I'm going here? These budget "buckets" are not just about saving money and spending within your means (although that's a huge benefit, too). They allow you to set boundaries on your actions and encourage you to be intentional with your purchases, while constantly forcing you to remember what matters most when it comes to your finances. They're gentle reminders to fight the impulsive urge to spend, egged on by the advertising messages with which we're constantly bombarded. Setting up well thought out monthly spending categories helps us learn the difference between want and need. And far from being merely restrictive, they're getting us to a place of freedom, space, and choice.

The Privilege of Spending

While we're talking budgeting and finances, I'd like to be clear that we're talking about consumer debt—debt we choose to take on. I realize that there are much bigger systemic and situational reasons for the accumulation of debt that have absolutely no relation to the type of debt we're talking about here. Right now, we're talking about the purchases we've made that were unnecessary and served to get us into debt—like those unnecessary Target hauls or Starbucks lattes we threw onto a credit card, knowing there wasn't enough money in the checking account to cover it. Quite simply, the spending discussed here is when we purchased things we didn't need with money we didn't have.

I've carried my fair share of consumer debt in the past. I've racked up credit card bills, paid them late, and had the credit score to show for it. That debt wasn't *necessary* debt—it was *emotional* debt. It wasn't about my inability to do the math and balance my checkbook; it was a conscious choice to disregard my current financial situation and instead make a purchase to fill an emotional void. I bet if you're reading this, you've done (or are doing) the same. As consumers in our society, we constantly justify making purchases we can't afford because we see everyone around us doing it, too. And it needs to *stop*. If you want a simpler life, you must stop justifying your emotional needs and allowing them to control your financial decisions.

Getting out of debt and breaking the mindless cycle of emotional spending isn't easy. And it's not something you can change overnight. But like everything else, it's about baby steps. You didn't get to this point in a few days—it's probably been an accumulation of unnecessary purchases over the years. And it's going to take months, or even years, to undo the damage. But the freedom that comes with it is priceless. And it's a privilege. Right now, there are people all over the world who simply cannot afford the basic necessities of life. Find gratitude in all you are fortunate enough to have, and you'll be ready to ditch the unnecessary debt once and for all.

LIVING WITH LESS

So you've figured out what your priorities are from a spending perspective. You know where you want your money to go. And you've reworked your budget so that what you're bringing in is meeting your needs, funding your dreams, and providing you with the power and freedom that being in control of your finances in a simpler way offers. You're probably feeling pretty good about all of that, and for good reason. I bet it's removed a sense of powerlessness and stress from the equation, because now your priorities are aligned across more areas of your life. Want to graduate to the next level and step up your game when it comes to living minimally? Here's some ways to take it even further, incorporating some of my favorite tips for even simpler finances. Let's start with my favorite little tip: Try living with less.

No-Spend Sessions

My first taste of living with less was when I stumbled upon the popular trend of "no-spend" challenges. Contrary to the name, the concept of no-spend months doesn't mean not spending any of your money. Instead, no-spend sessions are the opportunity to go without the simple pleasures that we've often become accustomed to in our daily spending. This isn't deprivation; it's just taking a small break from some truly unnecessary spending behaviors and habits that we've all become used to. It's simple, temporary changes—like passing on that dress you've been eyeing that's now on sale. It's bypassing a salon pedicure and instead doing your toes at home with polish you already have, or using up that flour, tomato sauce, and cheese you've already got in your pantry and fridge to craft a homemade pizza instead of ordering takeout. It's giving up what you *want* to purchase for a month and spending your money only on what you *need*. You get the point. It's giving yourself the time and space to live in a little bit of discomfort and really examine whether those "splurges" bring you as much happiness as you imagined—or if perhaps the free, substitute versions can bring you just as much joy.

It's totally okay if after making it through a no-spend week or month, you find that you desperately miss those simple pleasures. It's not about depriving yourself of all the little things that bring you happiness; in fact, simple living is about embracing those very things. It's about making those little moments and experiences and those everyday luxuries a priority. If you end up finding you can do without, great. You've further explored what brings you joy and what's just become a habit. And if you truly realize you find true happiness in that small luxury, you've gained a newfound and more conscious appreciation for it in your life. Either way, you've clarified what matters most to you when it comes to where you spend your money—a critical component to simpler spending.

Not Keeping Up with the Joneses

Today's society makes it so incredibly easy to play the grass-is-always-greener game. With visual access to everyone's lives with the simple tap of a screen, we're handed a weighty, dangerous serving of jealousy and comparison that we often didn't ask for. It's easy to spend a few minutes daily checking out everyone else's highlight reels and instantly feeling the need to acquire a better home, better wardrobe, better makeup bag, or better cleaning routine.

Recognize it. Feel it. And then let those feelings pass.

One of the hardest things about living more simply is learning to let that feeling of inadequacy go. I hate to break it to you, but there will always be a bigger home; a better kitchen; a brighter complexion. No matter what you do, you'll never be the best. You'll never be on top. You'll never "win" that game. And guess what? That's life. When you learn to let the need to run that race go, you'll start noticing that what you've already got is pretty amazing, exactly as it is.

Don't get me wrong, the desire to want better is an admirable thing. Don't mistake what I'm saying for settling for mediocrity. I'm talking about the artificial, inflated need to have better or be "better" simply because you're able to peer into the lives of other people on an incredibly ridiculous scale these days. You do *you*, and revel in all that your life is. Don't let your satisfaction with what you've got going on be wrecked by taking a peep into someone else's life. It's totally human nature. But recognizing it and letting it go is crucial to a simpler life full of satisfaction. The sooner you can recognize those feelings when they come up and let them pass, the sooner you can move on with your day and find all the joy that's waiting for you in the life you've already worked so hard to create.

Self-Control is Sexy

What's more attractive than self-control? It's a powerful tool—one that we reward endlessly when it comes to diet or exercise, cleaning routines, or sleep schedules for our children. So why not your finances, too? Saving is an undeniable form of self-control that provides you with one of the ultimate forms of security. Creating and maintaining a budget is proof that you trust yourself: proof that you stand behind your word. It's pride in sticking to and chasing after a goal that matters to you. It's a plan, something that will help you get to your end goal without floundering aimlessly along the way or winging it and hoping for the best. It's a sign that you're both prioritizing those tangible and experiential things in life that matter most to you, as well as building a secure foundation for yourself, your family, and your future. And it's those small sacrifices, those little, incremental changes we make, that add up to truly lasting change.

Simplifying Isn't Settling

Yes, budgeting often means doing without. It means watching what comes into our home. It sometimes involves hand-me-downs, or buying secondhand, which are all well and good. To lead a simpler life, I try to limit my purchases. I try to be resourceful with what's already in our home. And I do my best to be grateful and work with what I already have, or what's most practical or useful.

But it doesn't have to be that way *all* the time, because simplifying your life does not mean you have to settle for something that doesn't benefit you and your family; it actually means the total opposite. Go spend a few extra dollars on something that works better for you if it means streamlining your life, removing stress, eliminating frustration, or just treating yourself. I'm not encouraging you to go spend money that you don't have available. Rather, I'm asking you to be a good steward of your finances and to allocate your funds to those areas that will bring a maximum return on investment when it comes to your daily joy.

Because sometimes, an item just makes sense—or saves your sanity. Sometimes, it's one of those unicorn purchases that covers both of those bases. And you check your bank account, look at your budget, and then go ahead and make that purchase without guilt. And you sing a little hallelujah that such a miracle object exists.

I get it: Budgeting is not glamorous; in fact, it's quite the opposite. It requires analytical thinking, digging deep to figure out where you want to spend your *time* and balancing that with where you want to spend your *money*. It's a delicate dance of making sure that everything aligns on the financial front to ensure one less stress sits on your shoulders every day. It's work, as most things worth attaining are. And it may seem like a "later" task for you: an item you'll get to once you simplify your stuff. But let me tell you, it's not just about getting rid of debt (although that's a wonderful side effect of all of this). It's about getting rid of the societal constructs we've encountered and the internal stories we've told ourselves thus far in our lives. It's about embracing a different, alternate path; the road less traveled.

But according to Robert Frost, isn't that the one that made all the difference?

Embrace "Enough"

Repeat after me: I have what I *need.*

It's taken me years to learn what "enough" looks like for me. And it's been a struggle. The purging part of minimalism and simpler living? That was easy. It was relatively easy for me to sell or donate all the excess in our home, because it's freeing—the sense of space that's left when the unnecessary departs and what remains has room to breathe.

But the key to simpler living? It's finding contentment in living with "enough."

It's hard to break that pattern of amassing more things. It's out there, everywhere—messages tempting you to buy more things you don't need; to stock up on items while they're on sale; to purchase multiples of everything, just in case; or to eye that handbag, or those kitchen countertops, or that shiny new car, and think you *have* to have it. But letting go of that urge for all the "extra" has changed my life. Not filling that space within my home, my head, and my heart, and holding tight to the knowledge that I've already got everything I need? It's liberating in the most unexplainable way.

Enough looks different for every single one of us. And it changes, too, with each season of motherhood. But learning to leave that space—in my cabinets, my days, and what I choose to consume— opens the door for a life of contentment and freedom that nothing else can provide. It's a privilege to be able to choose "enough" for my life.

Be brave enough to choose it for yours, too.

CHAPTER 5

A Simpler Kitchen

Welcome to my kitchen.

The counters here hold more than you'd imagine for a minimalist. There are large glass crocks of flour that we use almost daily to make homemade bread and muffins. A large silverware caddy corrals our cutlery and useful kitchen tools. A tiered metal tray holds all the aforementioned baked goods. A few large wood cutting boards spark joy every time I notice the contrast of their warm wood against all our white finishes. And there's a vase of fresh eucalyptus because...well, it just looks pretty.

And let me tell you, that's the true beauty of minimal living: You get to make your own beautiful kind of simple. There's no definition you must adhere to; no rules you must follow. You can have bare walls or tons of décor; empty, spacious drawers or neat, fully stocked and color-coded ones. Your dwelling can hold completely full bookcases or no books at all. Simple living is about curating a home intentionally and purposefully; keeping and acquiring the things that are used, loved, and appreciated daily, and letting go of the rest. It's about removing the burden of the unnecessary and freeing up all that time and energy for better things: playing, cooking, creating, loving...living.

When it comes to my kitchen, there's no rules on how it looks, only how it feels. Some seasons, it's pretty minimal—a few necessary items sit on the counters, and the rest get tucked neatly behind the cabinet doors. Other times, I feel the need for a more lived-in, loved-on vibe, and out come pitchers of greens and seasonal décor. In some seasons of life, I savor the amazingness that comes with a freshly brewed cup of coffee from our French press, which stores neatly out of sight and off the countertops after breakfast. Other times, I whip out our Nespresso and survive that phase of newborn exhaustion with an additional appliance that becomes a semi-permanent fixture on our countertops. But regardless of how much or how little lives in my kitchen, it still feels minimal because it only includes items that bring me joy and help me function in that space. And it's easy to keep clean—just a few minutes at the end of the day, and we're back to even; simple and sanity-saving, even on the worst of days.

A huge part of creating a simpler kitchen is learning that it doesn't need to be perfectly beautiful to be incredibly useful. As a stay-at-home mom of four, I spend the majority of my days in or passing through this crucial room in our home. It's the first room I enter at the beginning of my day and the last room I exit at the end of it. It's a crucial space in our home, however imperfectly laid out or outdated it may be. And learning to view it as a space that functions and serves me as a mother has been crucial to my ability to declutter, streamline, and rediscover the joy within its walls.

— — —

There are many reasons why your kitchen may very well be top of the list when it comes to the spaces in your home that most need simplification. As a newly minted minimalist a few years back, it was the first space I wanted to streamline for a few very important reasons.

For one, our kitchen was short on storage space. I simply couldn't fit in everything I'd amassed for myself, my four kids, and my exceedingly haughty notions of becoming a master chef. I'd spent years acquiring new gadgets that promised to make my life as a mom easier. I'd held onto the pots and pans and those five random spatulas from my college days, hesitant to part with them. I mean, what if I needed them? And most importantly, I'd bought into the popular notion that I needed to buy in bulk to save money, which meant stocking our pantry to the brim with food that inevitably expired before it got eaten.

Secondly, it was the space I used the most during the day. It was the one that provided a daily headache when the dishes wouldn't fit, preventing the cabinet door from closing. It held the drawer I spent a good five minutes furiously rooting through every time I went looking for that storage container's lid. It was the space where I spent the bulk of my day—cooking, cleaning up, washing dishes, and entering and exiting. And guess what? It absolutely drove me nuts.

Crafting a simpler kitchen encompasses so much more than just clearing out your junk drawer and organizing your pantry (although we'll tackle those projects in this chapter, don't worry). But a simpler kitchen goes beyond the superficiality of streamlined systems and organized cabinets. It's about learning to create simpler meal planning, cooking routines, and grocery shopping skills, as well as focusing on quality over quantity. Keep it simple—especially with young kids. And most importantly, rediscover the immense joy that can come from creating and preparing food to feed and nourish the ones you love most. It's truly the heart of so many homes—whether you're a busy working mom with a crazy schedule, a stay-at-home mom eager to make all the things from scratch, or somewhere in between.

CREATING A KITCHEN YOU LOVE

It's your kitchen. Love it, hate it—or somewhere in between—it still needs to serve you. And the easiest way to begin removing the chaos that often comes from a workhorse of a space in our homes is by removing the excess and holding on to only the items that get used, are loved, and serve you. The more use a space gets in your home, the more important this concept becomes.

There is no one way to go about streamlining and minimizing your kitchen—or any other space, for that matter. For years, I assumed that I needed to follow a certain protocol or structure to declutter successfully. But like any other end goal in life, no one else's routine or method is going to work perfectly for everyone. We're all different, and so are our spaces. So sure, there are certain tips, tricks, and ideas that you can borrow from others. But don't get so fixated on following someone else's process that you forget to edit it and make it your own. I follow a few loose concepts each time I declutter, but that doesn't mean they'll work for you. They're outlined below, but as always: Take from these ideas what works for you, and discard the rest. Some may be super helpful; others may not work for you and your space. It's a trial-and-error kind of thing, the kind that only ends up being successful if you take the time to learn what works best for you and what doesn't. And the only way to figure that out is to do the work.

IT GETS WORSE BEFORE IT GETS BETTER

I'm sure you've heard it said or experienced it firsthand before, but any good decluttering or reorganizing project is going to create a bigger mess than the one you started with. It's painful; it's demotivating. It can be super overwhelming. But it's *necessary*. In order to figure out what you need and what you don't, you need to get every single item that belongs in that space out and make it visible. I know, that sounds crazy, but it's critical. You need to be able to physically see everything you're expecting to go into that space in order to truly determine what you need and to prioritize what truly belongs there.

So roll up your sleeves. Go around to your other rooms and gather any possible item you think may end up in that kitchen space. Storage baskets, wedding china, your weekly planner—it all needs to go in the kitchen. Go ahead and pull every single item out of your pantry and cabinets and place it all in a space where it can be sorted through easily. That may be right on your kitchen counters. Maybe it's your kitchen floor. Heck, you might need to take over your dining room table (if there isn't already a pile of stuff growing on it!) to get it all together.

See what I mean? You're making a bigger mess than you started with, but I promise it's going to turn out better than you anticipated.

Group Items Together

Now that you've got everything out in view, it's time to do the hard work. This is the part of the process that usually takes the most time, but it's also the part where you'll start to clearly identify what matters most to you. I want you to start grouping all your items together. All your pantry goods and staples? Put them in one big pile. All your cooking utensils? They go in a pile, too. Your plates, cups, and dishes? Place them all together. Your pots, pans, and cookware? Yep, it all gets grouped.

Go through all your items until they're all in relatively similar groupings. Don't take too much time worrying about the "right" group an item belongs in. Just go with your first gut instinct and move on. We've got a lot more work to do, and the objective isn't to label your items into the proper categories—that's just a tool to help you start to clearly see where the unused, the excess, and the unnecessary lie, and to make it much easier to part with anything that's just cluttering up your kitchen and adding chaos to an already-busy space.

It's probably a lot, huh? Good. Now, let's start decluttering.

Keep, Donate, Sell, or Trash

Now that you've got everything in groups, you're going to spend some time really analyzing what each item in those groups means to you. We're going to group those items into three categories: keep, donate, sell, or trash. Remember that your donate or sell pile isn't immediately leaving your home (unless you're ready for it to go!), it's just going into your storage purgatory to see if you truly still need it in your life. This should be easy work. Either you love it and use it (keep), it's broken or unusable (trash), or it falls somewhere in the middle (donate or sell).

I know that decision-making process isn't easy for everyone, so let's talk about how to get there.

Got three whisks? It's a common thing to have multiples of the same item. Now let's do a deep dive into how each of these items—in this instance, a whisk—functions and is needed in your home. How often do you really use a whisk more than once a day? I bet one is your favorite, and you use that one every single time you bake or whip up some scrambled eggs. So let me ask you...why are you holding onto the other two?

Maybe one was a gift, but you hate the way the handle feels. Or you bought the other one years ago and spent a lot of money on it, but it has a wooden handle and can't go in the dishwasher, so you never use it. Whatever the reason is, it doesn't serve you anymore! It's literally sitting in a drawer, adding clutter to it. Let. It. Go.

Same goes for Tupperware without a coordinating lid; that coffee mug you got in Florida that sits in the back of your cabinet; or that expired jar of pasta sauce from 2016 that's been hiding in the back of your pantry—just in case. None of that is useful or beautiful to you. And it's certainly not doing anything to benefit you in any way. In fact, it's probably in the way every single time you open a door to a cabinet in your kitchen, preventing you from more easily accessing the things you actually use. It's just making your day harder and more stressful *every single time you go to do something in your kitchen.*

Nobody has time for that. Especially a busy mother.

House the Less-Used Elsewhere

Does that reframe things in a different way for you? If you want a simpler, cleaner, more organized and less cluttered kitchen (or any space for that matter), you must let go of things that are barriers to the way you function. Keeping those extra dishes you rarely use in your main dish cabinet doesn't just add clutter, it makes getting to the dishes you *do* use harder and more stressful. Really think about that. If you and your family members eat three meals a day at home, that's three times *every single day* that you're reaching around that stack of unused dishes or sorting through them to get to the dish you need—three times *every single day* that you're inconvenienced, if only for a second, to accomplish a necessary task. Now multiply that by each cabinet, drawer, or space in your home that has extra items cluttering the space and preventing you from moving through your day with a little more ease and a lot less stress. Seems silly to keep moving around those obstacles, right?

We need to put that stuff somewhere else. Listen, I get it. There are plenty of items in my home that I don't use every day, but that I still love, or utilize on a less frequent basis. I'm not going to get rid of them for the sake of minimizing my space, because guess what? I'd be out borrowing or purchasing them the next time I needed them. But guess what? They also don't need to occupy precious real estate where they take up valuable space and make my daily tasks more frustrating. So I store them elsewhere.

There's no rule that every item you *use* in your kitchen needs to *live* in your kitchen. This goes for every other space in your home, too! I don't know why we expect each item we own to fit neatly into this perfect little package—life certainly doesn't work that way. Don't use your entertaining china or muffin tins more than a few times a year? Get them out of your kitchen cabinets and store them elsewhere. Maybe it's a closet, the top shelf of your pantry, the basement storage room, or even a makeshift buffet in your living room (my own personal method!). It takes only a minute to walk to another room and grab the item I need just a few times a year, which sure beats moving around it to get to what I use *every single day*. Think outside the box. Is there a room or space that you can use? Do it! Free up that precious kitchen space by keeping your seldom-used items in storage. You don't have to get rid of it to live simpler, you've just got to think smarter.

MAKE IT PRETTY

You know how the icing on the cake is the prettiest, most fun part of baking? Or how putting on your jewelry and adding some makeup is the best part of getting dressed up? Same goes for simplifying and decluttering.

You've purged. You've edited. You've gotten rid of what you don't use. You've rehomed the occasional items. And you're left with the items that bring you joy; the ones that serve a purpose and help make your kitchen work for you. Now what? Now comes the fun part: We get to make it pretty. Hey, you didn't think I'd just tell you to cram it all back into your cabinets, did you?

You've got your items grouped. Now, we're going to put them back in a format that makes your kitchen work for you—in a functional way that makes sense. Your coffee cups probably need to go in a spot close to your coffee maker. Your dishes should probably be put away in a cabinet close to your dishwasher or sink. And your cooking utensils might serve you better in a simple crock on your countertop, right next to the stove. How you put that puzzle back together is up to you. And since you've removed the excess, you may end up having some extra space in and around your things. *Fight the urge to fill it*, because that blank space is a thing of beauty in and of itself. It breathes calm into your day every time you open a cabinet and see some empty space instead of a tower of tightly stacked dishes. Give your stuff that room to *breathe*.

But we're not stopping there. Now, we're also going to make it as pretty as possible. At this point, many decluttering and organizing coaches and professionals will tell you to go out and buy a whole bunch of new bins, baskets, and containers. And sure, if that's what you want to do and you have the budget to do so, go crazy! Have fun. Buy the prettiest organizers you can, and create the organized kitchen of your dreams. But also know that this isn't necessary, at all. Because we can still make this space functional—and beautiful!—without spending a dime. How? We're going to use what we have.

That's right. Get creative. Shop your home. And make use of what's already on hand. I bet you have a few mason jars lying around. Guess what? They make excellent storage containers for dry goods in your pantry or for storing freshly cut fruit in your fridge. I bet you have some empty cardboard boxes. Remove the lids or cut off the flaps. Voila! Free containment of your Tupperware lids or back stock items in your pantry. Those extra toy bins in the playroom or plastic storage bins in your medicine cabinet? Use those to contain the apples in your fridge, or that half eaten box of granola bars.

They don't have to cost anything, but storage vessels are your best friend. I'm a huge fan of decanting—an organizational trend that's all over social media these days. It makes everything simpler, less busy, and prettier. Simplified, decanting is basically taking items out of their cardboard or plastic containers and placing them into baskets, bins, or jars. It groups items by type and allows you to see exactly how much of an item you have on hand. It makes items easier to locate, and it prevents us from wasting things in our home. Sure, it looks gorgeous, too. But it's both a functional tool and a way to make things look pretty—and when you can combine the two, there's nothing better.

Again, you can go out and buy a whole bunch of expensive jars and storage containers if you want to, but it's not necessary. A pack of twelve mason jars costs less than ten dollars at most stores and can get you started on your path to pantry bliss. Empty spaghetti sauce jars can also do exactly the same, without spending an extra dime. Or shop your home—again, simple woven or plastic bins can help group, corral, and contain items in your kitchen to make your cabinets and drawers less cluttered.

Whatever you do, make it functional, and choose the storage and organizational methods that work for you. If you know you just don't have the time (or motivation) to decant items when you get home, ditch that concept! If the sight of perfectly filled glass jars of pantry staples makes your little heart flutter (guilty as charged!), then take the time to do it. There is no one way to create an organized, simple kitchen. Do what works best for you.

Now that you've got your kitchen put back together, let's tackle how to keep it simple in your day-to-day life; and more importantly, let's tackle how to keep your sense of perspective when your kitchen feels less than perfect.

LESS CLUTTER, LESS DIRT, MORE JOY

So your kitchen feels better. You've got more space. Things are organized. You can find what you need when you need it. It feels good, right? Excellent. Now let's step it up a level and talk about some simple ways to make clutter even less of an issue. Here are some of my favorite strategies to reduce it and make your space work for you. Again, take the ideas that work for your space and needs and pass on the rest. It's all about what's going to make your life easier.

Go Vertical

One of my favorite ways to utilize space in your kitchen without cluttering your countertops or cabinets is to add storage to your walls. Shelves and wall baskets are your best friend! They remove items like dishes, spices, and even fruit from taking up valuable space and instead utilize empty wall space already available in your kitchen. This is prime real estate, folks. On top of offering functional storage, it also looks really good. I mean, a hanging wall basket full of colorful fruit? It's practically a work of art. Combining beauty and function is the easiest way to make your house feel like a home. Plus, it helps prevent waste—having food out and in plain sight allows you to see what you have, add what's needed to your grocery list, and prevent easily perishable foods from going bad before they are used or eaten.

Vertical storage also works well for functional items like dishes, glasses, pots, pans, and even knives. There are tons of affordable solutions that allow you the ability to store items vertically and get them up off the countertops or out of your valuable drawer and cabinet space. You can even use clear jars or containers for pantry staples like flour, sugar, coffee, and baking ingredients, or even snack foods! Again, doing it that way prevents food waste and allows you to combine both beauty and function. Imagine not needing to buy any décor items or artwork to furnish your kitchen with a personal touch! It's a simple concept, but one that is super valuable in a space like the kitchen, where you access so many different items multiple times a day.

Contain, Contain, Contain

Bins, jars, and containers are a valuable tool when it comes to simplifying, organizing, and making your kitchen work for you. Sure, you could keep items stacked on top of and next to each other in your pantry, cabinets, and drawers. Or you can contain what's in there to make it look better and function in a less-cluttered way.

Again, you don't need to spend an entire paycheck at the Container Store to do this. Simple cardboard shipping boxes can easily go on top shelves and contain less-used items like pantry backstock, seasonal cooking tools or dishware, or even less used cookware. They also work extremely well to contain kids' sippy cups and dishes. Rather than assembling those sippy cups each time they're washed and wrangling all the seals, straws, lids and cups, you can just toss them in a basket and grab what you need when you need it. If you want to take it one step further, you can corral the individual pieces in smaller boxes or plastic bins within that larger bin so it's even easier to grab what you need when the kids are chirping for some water.

Baskets are also great to group similar items in the pantry. All the snack food boxes and bags can easily be corralled into one bin for easy access, and they can be kept at a level the kids can reach so they can begin to independently choose their snacks when the time comes. They also make meal planning easier. If you've got a bin for pastas, one for sauces, and another for canned veggies, you're able to easily figure out what to make for dinner for the upcoming week and add items that are needed to your grocery list, since you can inventory what you've already got on hand with one quick glance.

Containers in the pantry help streamline the clutter and make your space so much less visually cluttered. Again, it's up to you and the way you want your home to function. It may not be worth the trade-off to decant items into clear containers, or it may make total sense for your family and the season you're in. These ideas are all merely suggestions to help implement simple systems into your kitchen that can help make your daily time there a little less hectic and a little more enjoyable.

Wash More, Store Less

If you're anything like me, you probably have many more cups, plates, bowls, and utensils than people in your home. After all, most families purchase their dishware in sets of eight, ten, or twelve. Now, if you've got a large family, those dishes probably get used daily. But if your family is smaller, most of those dishes probably sit untouched in those cabinets. I bet you use the same six plates stacked on the top of your dish pile every single day. Am I right? The rest simply sit and gather dust at the bottom of the stack, only to be used on rare occasions.

With the invention of the dishwasher, most families can wash and reuse many of their items easily on a daily basis. So why are you renting storage space to all those unused items? Reduce the amount of dishware you store in your kitchen cabinets, and keep only the number of dishes you use daily. The rest can be donated, sold, or stored in a less-used space for entertaining or for when your family grows.

Our family of six has eight of each item in our cabinet. That's right—eight bowls, eight small plates, eight large plates, eight kids' plates, eight kids' bowls, and eight glasses in our dish cabinet, and that's it. I know that sounds crazy, but it's what we use! With the number of meals and snacks we prepare in a day, the dishwasher usually gets run at least once, so there's always a clean glass, bowl, or dish for use. Our extra dishware lives in a cabinet close by, but we only grab from it when we have guests to entertain. Ask me how many times I've had to run the dishwasher or wash a dish during the day because we've run out of clean dishes? Maybe once.

It's what works for us, and it clears up valuable space in our kitchen. I do the same with bakeware, pots, pans, and utensils. We don't need or use sixteen forks or spoons throughout the day. Eight of each cutlery item is plenty for us. By storing the rest out of the way, I'm not stuck rooting through a stuck drawer or overfull cabinet. Every item is touched and utilized daily. And it allows us to easily set up to entertain guests by simply running to another room and grabbing a few extra cups, plates, or dishes when the need arises. It seems like a simple concept, and per-haps it wouldn't make a big difference. But when you're digging through a drawer or opening a cabinet three times a day, having the space simplified makes such a huge difference. Try it out for a week; play with figuring out the amount of dishware and kitchen items your family truly needs, and decide for yourself if it's not worth keeping the excess items stored out of the way for those few times a year when you need them—or perhaps getting rid of them altogether.

Store Smart

Both being smart about how you store things in your spaces and organizing your items with function in mind are critical when creating a simple kitchen. It's a waste of your time and energy to place items in cabinets or drawers in ways that make your job harder. For example, placing dishes, glassware, and utensils all in the same "zone" within your kitchen makes the most sense for putting dishes away after washing as well as grabbing what's needed for each meal during the day.

It's also essential to get creative with your storage solutions. For example, we keep our cutlery and many of our serving and cooking utensils in caddies and crocks on our countertop versus crammed in drawers. Our kitchen is old and small—we have a total of three drawers in the entire space. Trying to fit all our cutlery and utensils in those drawers just didn't make sense, so I now store almost all of our cooking utensils in a large crock right next to the stove, and our cutlery is in a caddy on the countertop immediately below our dishes. It makes it super easy to grab exactly what we need when I'm preparing food or setting the table, and it frees up valuable real estate in those drawers for storing less-used kitchen items out of sight.

Organize your kitchen by thinking about zones. Establish a cooking zone where all your pots, pans, and cookware live. Keep all your pantry items together. Maybe keeping all your baking supplies in a cabinet near the stove makes the most sense. Think about how you function in your kitchen and what tools and items you use together often. Organize with intelligence, and your space will easily serve you in a more efficient, less stressful manner on a daily basis.

What are some areas where you can bring creativity and strategy to your kitchen organization? Examine your space; use a bit of trial and error to develop the most efficient storage solutions for it. There's no one right answer, either. As your kids grow, your needs (and your stuff) often change. Those sippy cups won't be there forever; and your kitchen storage needs will change just as your family does. Be ready to edit your kitchen storage system seasonally—whether that means with each actual season during the year, or perhaps less often, with each season of motherhood as you journey through it. Either way, flexibility is key. Be aware that the systems you create are not a one-and-done kind of thing—they will evolve and change. Be prepared to put a little ongoing work into reevaluating your space, being realistic about what truly is needed—and what actually fits—into that kitchen.

Store It in the Sink

Visual clutter can be just as stressful as physical clutter. You may have simplified your kitchen, but there will be very few times when it's not in use. Cluttered countertops can cause immediate anxiety and chaos for me, but I can't spend my entire day tidying up my kitchen—it's just not realistic. So I employ one of my favorite tricks during the day when things are often either dirty, or drying, or in the process of being prepared or cooked: I store them in the sink. Whether you have a shallow, two-basin kitchen sink or a glorious, deep, single basin one (hello, heaven!), make it your mission to store everything that would normally clutter up your countertops in the sink.

You heard that right. Got a bunch of bottle parts and sippy cups air drying? Find a sink basin rack and let them air dry out of sight. Or simply move your countertop drying rack into the sink, eliminating its visual clutter. Same goes for dirty dishes—you don't need to immediately rinse dishes and get them loaded in the dishwasher! Instead, I let them pile up a bit in my kitchen sink. Make sure you place them in there in a somewhat organized manner for easier loading later—think stacking plates together, bowls together, and then storing all silverware in a single glass or mug so you're not stuck digging through topsy-turvy dirty dishes when you go to load the dishwasher at the end of the day or when the sink ends up too full. It's my version of working smarter, not harder in the kitchen, and it completely eliminates that chaotic feeling of constant clutter when I pass through during my day.

Get In Your Groove

Find systems and loose routines that work for you when it comes to your daily kitchen chores. Combining your efforts will not only make your life easier, but it will also save you time when it comes to cleaning your kitchen and keeping things organized through-out the day. For me, there's several easy systems I've created that make my life easier and simplify my efforts in the kitchen.

For example, we load the dishwasher at the end of every day and let it run overnight. In the morning, I unload it while I'm already in the kitchen, waiting for my coffee to brew. It starts the day off on the right foot by immediately completing a necessary task, and it allows me to quickly load dishes as the kitchen sink piles up. Knowing that one of my kitchen chores is done within the first few minutes of the day—and knowing that the dishes will be clean by morning—eliminates the task of cleaning dishes for the rest of the day. I simply let my sink fill, then load the dishes. The calm that comes from that simple habit frees up so much time and energy to focus on other, more important and enjoyable components of my life as a mom.

Most importantly, feel free to create a kitchen that feels good to you. For you, that may mean cleaning the countertops and sweeping the floors at the beginning or end of every day, or cleaning the kitchen on the same day every week. Myself, I like to tackle tasks when I have the time and energy. I tried for years to adhere to a daily checklist or a weekly chore day, and doing it that way immediately added stress and pressure and made me feel like a failure if those tasks weren't accomplished. Instead, I now clean things as they need it, and as I have the time and energy to do it. My floors might be a bit stickier than yours. The countertops may not glisten in the sunlight every morning. But knowing that it'll get done when it's needed beats feeling obligated to routinely tackle things just for the sake of a system or to-do list. And that breathes simplicity into my life more than any cleaning routine ever could.

That being said, a simple home is also about caring for and maintaining what you have. I'm not asking you to give up caring about how clean things are, I'm asking you to be realistic about what is achievable and what you're able to maintain on a day-to-day basis based on the lifestyle within your home and the season of motherhood that you're in. Simple living is about ditching the pursuit of perfectionism and constantly wanting better, and instead embracing the beauty of your reality. And it's a heck of a lot easier to embrace the joy in what you already have if you take pride in it and care for it.

You don't need a brand-new kitchen full of new appliances to find joy, you just need to care for that old stove. Keep it clean; treat it with respect. Find value in what that stove does for you! It helps provide meals to feed your family every single day—whether it's a top-of-the-line gas range or a sixty-year-old electric one. Find joy in what your current situation is. Embrace the function it provides for you. And instead of neglecting what you have while you dream of that newer, better thing, start putting some time and energy into maintaining what's already working well for you. It costs you absolutely nothing and will breathe new life into how you feel every time you go to use it.

So we've decluttered your kitchen. We've chatted about the best ways to organize it. We've made it more functional, and we've developed simple routines and systems that work best for your family. Fantastic! Once you've figured out what works best for you and gotten everything put away, stand back and marvel at it.

Because it probably won't be that way for long.

I know that's not what you want to hear, but that's the reality. Your house is a *home*, which means it gets lived in, used, and messed up. And that's a beautiful thing. Treasure it—soak it in. Revel in its imperfection. I'm told there will be a time in the near future when I'll look back and yearn for those sticky handprints, rogue cheerios under the cabinets, and splattered applesauce all over again. That idea sounds crazy, but I get it. This season of motherhood is messy, but it's also short-lived. Enjoy the ride while you can.

As a mom, your kitchen will be used often—including by small children. Embracing a simpler kitchen is just as much about embracing it in its imperfection as it is about creating the perfect organized space. Motherhood is a constantly evolving season of life, full of baby bottles, drying racks, and towers of sippy cups. It's about spilled milk, sticky floors, and crumbs on the counters. The sooner you embrace that and stop trying to keep everything perfect throughout the day, the sooner you'll find the beauty in it.

No, your kitchen won't always be perfectly organized and clean. But clean-ish? Organized-ish? Simple-ish? That's what we're going for here. So instead of setting your expectations and standards at a sky-high level that's impossible to attain, let's embrace good enough. Let's keep in mind that while we've drastically simplified our kitchen, simple doesn't mean perfect. It means less of the excess, more of the good stuff, and the ability to live life in the best way possible, imperfectly happy.

CHEF'S KISS (KEEP IT SIMPLE, STUPID)

We've created a kitchen space that is simpler, more organized, and a heck of a lot more functional for you. But it's still just a space. In order to make it work even better for you, we need to talk more about the tasks we perform in the kitchen every day. After all, a kitchen's main function is to store the items that aid us in feeding ourselves, right? So, let's discuss the important actions that go into those efforts: meal planning, grocery shopping, and meal preparation.

Meal Planning

"Hey, Mom. What's for dinner?" Oh, meal planning. As mothers, this is most likely one of the biggest tasks we're charged with accomplishing on a weekly basis. It's something I both love and hate to do, often at the exact same time. With small kids, planning meals that stay within budget, are easy to prepare, and appeal to everyone in the family is a big challenge. For years, I failed miserably at this, because I either over planned or under planned. Or I didn't have a plan at all—all bad ideas. It's taken time and a lot of trial and error, but I've developed a few uncomplicated systems that have made meal planning a whole lot easier and less stressful. Below is the simplified meal planning process that I follow every week. Again, this is what I've found to work best for me—yours may look completely different. But finding ways to borrow concepts from others that make our own tasks and lives simpler is the whole point. Take what will help, discard what won't, and stop dreading your weekly meal planning!

Step One: Look at Your Calendar

Before you jump to picking meals and making a grocery list, it's critical to examine your schedule and see what it looks like. Some people love planning out an entire month of meals at one time, which can often help when it comes to staying on budget, as well as only having to tackle the task just once each month. Personally, I prefer to plan on a weekly basis. For one, I like the flexibility of being able to more easily change up what's for dinner without wasting food if our schedule changes—and with young kids, that happens quite often.

Secondly, I prefer to be able to change my mind on what's for dinner if the mood strikes. With weekly meal planning, I can edit my plans and adapt our week's meals to my family a bit more easily. I much prefer eating in this intuitive way rather than sticking to a month's worth of scheduled meals and not having a ton of flexibility to change my mind. When it comes to food, I enjoy variety, and the ability to change things up week-to-week makes preparing meals a much more enjoyable experience for me, rather than just a necessity.

And thirdly, I prioritize fresher, more produce-rich meals. Again, this is my own personal choice, but the seasonality of produce often changes quickly, especially during the summer months. And although frozen and canned fruits and vegetables are readily available, I prefer the real, in-season deal. Weekly planning allows me to flex our meal plan based on what's ripe, what's in season, and what's freshest. I'm much more likely to eat a fresh, new, seasonal meal and to enjoy the experience than to stick to a meal plan that relies on more shelf-stable or less perishable ingredients. Again, it's up to you how you choose to plan your meals, so choose a method that works for your family. Don't rely on someone else's system to work for you because quite often, it won't.

Once I've taken a look at my calendar, I figure out exactly how many meals I'll need to plan for the week. This prevents waste and allows me to make sure to only purchase the ingredients and items we need for the week. It also helps to know what activities and meals we'll be working around. Soccer practice on Tuesday night? We may pick up takeout on the way home since I won't have enough time to prepare a meal. The weather forecast calls for rain all week? Probably not a good idea to plan on a meal that requires grilling some of the ingredients. Family dinner with Mom and Dad on Sunday? We won't need to make dinner at home but may have to prepare a side dish to bring. Looking at what's on the agenda for the week allows you to more accurately gauge how many and what types of meals are going to be most successful for you and your family.

Step Two: Use What You Already Have

Now that you've looked at your calendar and you know how many and what type of meals you need to prepare for the week, take inventory of what you've already got on hand in the fridge, freezer, and pantry. Is there some lettuce that needs to get used in the next few days? You better believe a salad is going on the menu. Are there five cans of tomato paste that are almost expired? I'll probably add in a dinner with some sort of tomato-based sauce like jambalaya or spaghetti. Too many frozen foods crammed in the freezer? Let's use some of those up this week and make dinner easier on a busy night.

Whatever the ingredients or items may be, try to plan meals around what you've already got on hand. Not only does this save you money by reducing the number of items you'll need to purchase for the week, it also helps prevent an overstuffed pantry, fridge, or freezer and limits food waste. Sure, it's fun to plan a whole new week's worth of meals with new ingredients, but it's a lot more practical to use what you've already bought with your hard-earned money.

Step Three: Review Your Budget

Now that you've checked your calendar and taken inventory of what you have on hand, let's look at your grocery or food budget. Each week, I try my best to plan to spend roughly around the same amount on groceries (or less). This keeps me on budget for the month and allows me to plan meals more realistically. If we're under budget, I have a little more leeway when it comes to choosing meals—I can include those with a few more ingredients, or more expensive options. If we're trending toward being over budget for the month, I try to cut corners on our grocery spending when I can. Maybe that means aiming for one less meal with a meat component (often an easy way for us to save some money) or simply downgrading our ingredients; frozen fruit is usually less expensive than fresh fruit, for example. It's these small tweaks that help me shop successfully while also selecting nourishing meals that will fit into our schedule.

I know it seems like a lot of work at first, but once you get the hang of things, it becomes second nature. I don't need to consciously think about it anymore—it's just become a simple system I use whenever completing this weekly task, and it keeps things low-waste, functional, space-saving, and on budget around here. And to me, that's the key to simpler living: coming up with systems that feel effortless and help you achieve your goals.

Step Four: Set the Bar Low

You know how many meals and what types of meals you need to make. You also have a list of ingredients that need to be used. Now comes the fun part: creating your plan for the week. If you've ever been down the Pinterest rabbit hole or combed through your own personal stack of cookbooks, you've been bombarded with meal ideas. Everything looks good! And it's easy to get overzealous and want to make all these amazing, yummy-looking meals. But before you do that, let's take a step back and be realistic in our meal planning endeavors. The key to simple meal planning is a combination of a few basic goals that I aim to achieve every week.

Try One New Thing

For starters, I do my best to make only one new meal a week. The rest of the meals I plan are those I know are family favorites, ones that I've successfully executed before. I know it's tempting to try new things, and I encourage you to try things out, but in a small, low-risk way by only attempting one a week. If it's a huge success, you've got another meal to add to your go-to arsenal. If it's a flop, you only wasted your money, time, and energy on one meal that week.

Plan a Clear-Out-the-Fridge Night

One of the easiest ways I've found to make my weekly meal planning simpler, save myself time and money, and please my kids is to plan for one Clear Out the Fridge Night each week. We almost always have food left over after dinner, and although we sometimes eat leftovers for lunch, I'm not a huge fan of eating the same thing the following day—I like to change it up a little. Over the course of the week, leftovers pile up. One night each week (usually a busy evening, or right before I'm planning to grocery shop for the following week), I'll pull them all out and let everyone have their pick of what leftovers they'd like for dinner. My kids absolutely love this smorgasbord-style dinner, and it requires nothing more than heating up already prepared leftovers for a few minutes. If needed, I'll fill in the gaps with some additional chopped fruit here, or some yogurt or applesauce there, but either way, it helps cut down on my efforts and reduces (and often completely eliminates) wasted food, as well as saving us the money we'd otherwise be spending to cook or order another meal.

So. Stinking. Easy.

Mind the Deconstruction Zone

If you've ever tried to feed a two-year-old an adventurous new meal, chances are you know: The struggle is *real*. The reality of motherhood and feeding little ones is often that most of your efforts are in vain. That doesn't mean that you should throw up your arms and feed them chicken nuggets or macaroni and cheese for the next few years (although trust me—those are definitely staples around our home). But it does mean that you need to be smart about your meal planning when you've got younger kids, picky eaters, or just a variety of different palates in your family. Welcome to the Deconstruction Zone: one of the easiest ways to ensure any meal you make will get eaten by all your family members—at least most of the time. It's a super simple concept, but one that has saved my sanity when it comes to feeding my kids.

It's draining to spend an hour in the kitchen preparing a healthy, home-cooked meal only to be met with whines that no one wants to eat it. By selecting meals that can be easily deconstructed into smaller components, each with less or different sauces or seasonings, you're ensuring that most of the meal won't go to waste, regardless of their preferences. For example, my husband and I love spicy foods. I probably make tacos (or some variation on them) for dinner at least once a week; fresh lime, tons of chili powder, and homemade pico de gallo or guacamole—yum. However, two of my kids currently have an aversion to all things spicy, and one hates tomatoes. By cooking the chicken or beef on its own without the spices and separating some out before seasonings are added in, I ensure that there's a protein at dinner that my kids will all eat. The pico sits in the middle of our table, and my tomato-loving girls can happily dunk their chips in the salsa while my oldest eats them plain. The toppings are all served a la carte so my kids can choose which ones they'd like on their plate and leave those they don't prefer. It's a simple solution, but it saves me a ton of time, money, and energy, and it almost entirely eliminates waste and whining. To any mom who's slaved away at dinnertime only to end up dumping half of it into the trash: You're welcome.

And before you say, "Hey, Emily. What about exposing your kids to new foods, or foods they don't like?" I get it; it's important to me to make sure my kids are given the opportunity to try foods that are out of their comfort zone. To accomplish this, I'll still put a small bite of the seasoned meat on their plates for exposure to a new taste (next to their familiar meal), but it allows me to feed my family while making one meal—not having to prepare a second, child-friendly one. I'm not big on forcing kids to try a bite; simply putting it on their plates gives them the autonomy to make decisions about food for themselves. And doing it this way saves me the time and energy of nagging them to try a bite. When they're ready, they try it. It's super simple, and to me, that's the best way to go with most things involving kids.

If you feel differently, by all means plan your meals in the way that best suits you. For some families, maybe making separate meals for the adults and the kids works. I get it—there are definitely nights where we've done that. If you prefer to feed your kids what you're eating and not cater to their preferences at all, I get that too. May I suggest at least making sure there's one item on the plate that you know they like? It'll save your sanity on a tough night when there's nothing else they're willing to try. Either way, make sure to plan your meals accordingly and be realistic about what types of meals everyone in the family will eat. It'll make dinnertime infinitely simpler and more joy-filled for you all.

Family Style for the Win

Another easy way to get your kids to eat what you've prepared for dinner is to present it in a way that gives them the control: family style. Our four kids are all six and under. Giving them choices and allowing them to make decisions for themselves goes a long way. By preparing the items and placing them in the center of the table on one big platter, they're able to pick what and how much they want to eat of each item, as well as serve themselves independently—another time and sanity saver.

Whether it's one simple platter or a whole series of bowls and serving plates, take a few extra minutes to plate your meals this way. As a parent, I'm sure you've experienced the up-and-down dance parents do from the dining table as kids constantly present their requests for another serving of this or that. Having all the food on the table eliminates this issue and allows the entire family to sit down and eat their meal together. I've also found it makes it much more likely for kids to not only try new foods, but also to serve themselves another serving versus quickly sliding down from the dinner table when their first portion is gone. If you've ever dealt with the whines of "I'm hungry!" an hour after dinner, you know this is a huge deal. It may mean a few extra dishes to wash, but it allows our family to enjoy our meals together so much more.

Be Prepared

In the kitchen, a little prep work on the front end makes life as a busy mom infinitely easier. Part of meal planning is making sure you've got the ingredients you need, sure. But it's also important to have things ready to go when it comes to throwing together meals and snacks. I'm not a huge fan of spending my Sundays prepping every single ingredient in my fridge for the week ahead, nor am I fond of pre-making meals or meal components. I personally think it's crazy to waste an entire day of free time. Whether you're a stay-at-home mom, a working mom, or somewhere in between, it seems counterproductive to spend a day of rest doing chores. If that's your cup of tea, more power to you—I realize not everyone has the luxury of unlimited opportunities to get things done around the house. But when it comes to prep work in the kitchen for meals and snacks, I prefer to take the work-smarter-not-harder route and simply spend a few minutes batching my efforts.

One of the biggest time savers I've found is to wash, slice, and store my produce all at one time. By throwing all my produce into a sink full of water with a splash of vinegar, letting it all soak, and then slicing and storing it all at once, I'm only spending a few minutes preparing all the fruits and veggies we need for the week. It requires no repeat sessions, all the fresh and healthy foods are available and ready to go when my kids ask for a snack, and

I'm more likely to make better decisions about the foods I put in my body when there's a mason jar full of bright, freshly washed berries sitting right there the minute I open the refrigerator.

While we're talking about food storage, get yourself some inexpensive mason jars and call it a day—no need for those cheap plastic food storage sets with flimsy lids that always manage to go missing, or wasteful plastic bags. Mason jars have been a godsend when it comes to keeping my fruits and veggies stored inexpensively and ensuring they're still good to eat for an entire week (or even two!). I've even tried the expensive glass storage containers, and mason jars keep my foods fresh for just as long. Again, you do you, but there's a safe, inexpensive, fruit and veggie storage solution just waiting for you at a cost of less than ten dollars if you're looking for it.

Cook Once, Eat Twice (or More!)

Want another easy way to make meals simpler? Double the recipe. Whenever I'm preparing pasta dishes, enchiladas, homemade pizza, or anything else that I know freezes well, I simply double the recipe. Although I spend a bit more on ingredients for that week, I'm getting two meals out of one round of cooking, spending the same amount of time it would take just to make one. If yours is a smaller family, go ahead and make a single recipe and just divide it into two dishes during cooking time or when you're done—one for now, one for later. Stick it in the freezer, and voila! You've got an easy dinner on your hands, just waiting for you on a busy night when you don't have the time to make a meal (or maybe just a night where you can't fathom doing more than throwing something in the oven).

Store Near the Floor

This next one may be a bit controversial, but I'm a huge fan of teaching my kids independence, even if it means a little more effort and frustration on the front end. I know a ton of parents who prefer keeping snacks out of reach of little hands, but I absolutely love storing our snack foods on pantry shelves that even my youngest can reach. Make sure they're in a shatterproof or plastic container (don't ask me how I learned this) and have a discussion around snack rules. In our home, our kids must ask and receive permission to have a snack. But once they've made a request and I've given them the green light, they're free to reach for a plastic bowl from a stack I store in the pantry at their level and fill it with the snack of their choice. I'm careful to only store snack foods they are able to have at all times, like crackers, pretzels, or dried fruit. Special snacks like candy or cookies are stored on higher shelves that are not within reach.

Same goes for our fridge. The bottom drawer is stocked with apples, oranges, and other whole fruits or other snack foods that need to be refrigerated. Juice pouches, yogurt, and cut veggies and fruit also live on the lowest shelf (which is still within reach for even our two-year-old).

Have we had accidental spills? Sure. Have I had sneaky toddlers get into snacks without asking? Absolutely. These are all lessons I'm totally willing to grow through in order for them to learn how to independently do things for themselves around the house. Not only does this empower them to have control over a daily task, but it also makes my life easier. Whether my hands are soaking wet mid-dishes or I'm busy nursing the baby, it allows them to have access to a snack at the appropriate time without me having to stop what I'm doing. With four young kids in the house, it just makes sense and works for us at this season in our lives—and I only anticipate it continuing as the kids grow older.

— — —

As you can see, a simpler kitchen is about far more than spotless, clutter-free countertops and a perfectly organized pantry. Your kitchen needs to work for you. Whether you're starting at the beginning and perhaps overwhelmed by the stress of it all, or you're a seasoned pro just looking for simple tips and tricks that may save you a bit more time and energy, I'm hoping this chapter sets you up for success when it comes to the room in your home you likely use the most. Take what works for you, pass on the stuff that doesn't, and walk away knowing that you're setting yourself up for a calmer, more enjoyable experience every time you set foot in your kitchen. Enjoy!

CHAPTER 6

Simpler Shopping

I have a confession: I've been an obsessive clean freak, organizer, and possession purger since the day I was born. It's in my bones; in fact, I'm pretty sure it's woven into my DNA and even my soul. As a toddler, I lined my toys up in rows, lines, and patterns and set my dollhouses up with perfectly arranged furniture, often without playing with the actual dolls.

In elementary school, I used to dress in one single color from head to toe. My mother called me the human crayon. I just figured it all matched if it was the same color family, and it made getting ready for school every morning infinitely easier. In high school, my own mother paid me my weekly allowance in exchange for help purging, cleaning, and reorganizing our linen closets, fridge, and pantry.

Heck, I'm still reminded by my siblings that I came home from my surprise eighteenth birthday party and decided to move all my bedroom furniture to the center of the room so that I could scrub down my baseboards. I even deep-cleaned our fridge and freezer in our temporary rental home three days after we brought home our first baby from the hospital. Cringe.

As a fully admittedly driven, intense, type A, all-or-nothing personality, dealing with things in a restrained manner has never come easy to me. Over the years, I've attacked every effort to clear clutter and purge my stuff with a headstrong zest, plowing through rooms like a bull in a china shop. You'd think I'd be a pro at this whole simple living, minimal lifestyle thing after years of that, right?

Nope. Somehow, I always came out the other end of my overzealous cleaning and decluttering whims with nothing more than a temporary fix. Sure, my rooms were cleaner. My fridge was more organized. My home held less stuff. But soon enough, that space quickly filled up again as I continued to bring more and more new things—sure to make me happier—into my life.

Does this sound familiar to you? I'm sure most of us have been through this before, and it's easy to see why. Our world bombards us with the constant message that we need more stuff to make life better. And although I'm fully aware that we can't just stop consuming altogether, the real key to *keeping* your home simpler relies on one thing: shopping intentionally.

SHOPPING INTENTIONALLY

Shopping intentionally is *hard*. Trust me, I've been there—with those bags and boxes of donations, breathing a huge sigh of relief as more things exited my home and provided some much-needed breathing space. It felt good, but it didn't solve my problem; it didn't make things simpler.

Why not? Because I wasn't following up and shopping intentionally when the time came to bring more things into my home.

For years, I prided myself on my expertise at decluttering and organizing. I don't mean to brag, but I'm pretty good at it. I'd declutter the same closets and drawers over and over again, standing back to admire my newly minimized spaces and vowing to keep them organized and simple. But I didn't do the *real* work—the *hard* work. *I didn't examine my shopping habits.* I'd see an ad or hear another mom raving about the next must-have product, and if it was in our budget—add to cart. I would do it without another thought.

Simple living and decluttering go hand-in-hand, but do you know what's also vitally important? Pausing. It's essential to pause to consider what is needed: a pause to digest my thoughts and to give my brain time to process whether my life and my space truly need the value that this "must-have" item claims to provide. Guess what? Most of the time, I change my mind.

Because most of the time, we don't really *need* all that stuff. In today's world of instant gratification, it takes more effort to pause and consider a purchase than it does to complete one. And until you learn to consume intentionally, to stop purchasing mindlessly and impulsively, the cycle will continue to repeat itself. Your home may end up decluttered and minimized for a short period of time, but eventually, you'll be doing the exact same thing with new stuff, weeks, months, or years later. It's simple math. You can't create more space in your home by removing old things and bringing in another round of new, shiny ones.

Intentional consumption takes time and practice. And it's undoubtedly a cycle of success and failure. I'm still learning, years later. I still make mistakes—consuming too much and purchasing without allowing time to consider the weight of my decisions (both figuratively and literally). But the minute I acknowledge my missteps and make a course correction, life becomes infinitely simpler again.

Just. Stop. Buying.

I know, it sounds easy. But have you ever stopped and realized how often you purchase items? I bet you can't remember the last time you went more than a day or two without buying something. And while we do need to acquire things to sustain our lives and our homes, there's a distinct difference between buying items because we *need* them and buying because we *want* them. Just try it. If you've never looked at your shopping habits from this perspective, I challenge you to take a week to intentionally purchase only items you truly need. I guarantee the items that come into your home are infinitely more intentional and useful when you take this approach.

I fully believe that life is about experiencing happiness and joy, and I also think purchasing items you want can absolutely provide that. But most times, we bring something we think we need into our home, and then immediately, we're on to the next. We don't take the time to enjoy the happiness that item brings; we simply move on to the next must-have item for another rush of dopamine, another short-lived surge of satisfaction. It's a vicious cycle for sure, and one that needs to stop if you're looking to simplify things. So what's the first step?

Slow Your Roll

The very first step to simplifying your shopping habits is to slow the cycle of bringing things into your home. The easiest way I've found to do this is the one-in, one-out rule. It's not at all a new concept—many other decluttering experts and minimalists use it daily. But it sure is effective, and for good reason. By only allowing yourself to bring an item into your house if another one leaves, you're forcing yourself to intentionally weigh the value of the potential addition to your home, as well as intentionally compare it to the items you already own.

Let's be clear: I'm not talking about the essentials like groceries, toilet paper, and other items that keep your home running and ensure your family is healthy and happy. I'm talking about things like another new shirt, a new throw pillow, or that new face scrub you're sure will entirely change your complexion. Want to bring those items in? Sure. Just know that something else must go.

Why does this work so well? It helps me constantly evaluate the items I'm holding onto. Is that face scrub that caught my eye really worth purchasing if it means tossing an almost-new tube of face scrub that I already have in my bathroom? Probably not. I'm betting I just bought that one I have a few weeks ago, hoping it would do the same thing. That's the point: to learn to pause, think about your choices, and examine the *why* behind those urges to buy.

Marketing teams and sales departments spend millions of dollars to convince you that you have a definitive need for their products. It's literally their full-time job to be as persuasive as possible when advertising their stuff. Remember that the next time you see a commercial, ad, or shelf display and instantly feel the pull or "need" for an item. By reminding yourself that you'll have to get rid of something you already own in order to acquire this new thing, you're intentionally considering and comparing the value of spending money on the new thing versus using something you already have. This has saved me from "accidentally" purchasing something, like a new set of dish towels, when I've got a set that still has the tags on it sitting in my kitchen drawer (ask me how I know). Ever done something like that before? Yeah, it isn't helping you at all.

Save It for Later

You're browsing online, or you're shopping in a store, and you find something you really love. You want it. You need it. You *have* to have it. Great! It's always exciting to find things that you know are going to bring joy to your life or your home; things that will make your life better, easier, or more beautiful. But that doesn't mean you need it right this minute. One of the easiest ways to stay on budget, make sure you're purchasing intentionally, and still bring things you love into your home is to save items for later. What do I mean by that? I mean literally saving the item on a list, in a photo, or in your cart for later.

Here's how it works: If you're shopping at the store and you see an item that you're thinking will be a perfect addition to your home, take a photo of it or add the item to a wish list in your phone, and move on with the rest of your shopping. If you're shopping online, add it to your cart and then save it for later. Almost every major retailer now offers you the opportunity to do this directly on their website. If they don't, the in-person shopping rule applies—take a photo, or save the item to a list. You don't get to purchase it today, but it's still there, waiting for you to spend some time thinking on it.

At the end of the month, go back and look at your photos, or your list, or everything you've saved for later. I'm betting most of those items no longer seem like things you *have* to have, right? If they still do and you've got the money in your budget, by all means buy them! But I'm willing to wager that almost all those things no longer hold the value or appeal that they did when you first stumbled upon them. It's the way consumerism works—that initial high quickly fades. By coming back to make a more intentional decision a few days or weeks later, you remove the emotional pull from those purchases and you're able to shop from a more logical point of view. It gives you ownership over your consumption, rather than letting your impulses dictate what and how you buy.

When you're used to consuming impulsively, the shift to shopping intentionally is an empowering experience—one that you'll quickly embrace. Waiting on things is hard, I get it. We're wired to enjoy acquiring things because it feels good. And in society today, where extremely addictive and persuasive advertising bombards us everywhere we go, it takes even more self-control to step away. But knowing you're in control of your spending—even in a society that so hugely promotes consumption of material things—is a totally freeing experience. Just try it for a month and see how you feel.

You Can Always Change Your Mind

So you bought that thing. You thought you had to have it. Yet minutes after you get home and take that item out of the bag, that buyer's high is already gone. The excitement has disappeared, and you're quickly realizing that thing just isn't as necessary as you thought.

Guess what? You can always return it.

Today, almost every single store or business has a generous return policy that allows you to receive a full refund for your product, as long as it's still in the original packaging. Many stores even accept returns after a product has been used or opened! Know that you have the power to change your mind and the ability to return that item if you find it's just not going to serve you.

We're all human. We all need to acquire things. And often, even after delayed consideration, we make that purchase and bring that item into our homes and only then realize it's not exactly as wonderful or necessary as we thought. That is okay! No one is going to shop and consume perfectly. Embrace the process, honor the mistake, and take that item back. Get money back in your pocket and space back into your home, and remove the guilt and disappointment that comes with realizing you made a bad purchase.

I fully realize the economic impact that returning items (especially by mail) can have. But what's even worse in my eyes is holding onto a purchased item that you won't be using. Unless that thing is donated or rehomed, it will inevitably end up in a landfill. Not the ideal place for an item that could be used and appreciated by another consumer, right? I feel like a broken record at times saying this, but as always, a simpler life isn't about doing everything perfectly; it's about living life with a bit more intention so that we're making choices with our resources, our things, and our time that will benefit both us and the rest of our world for the years to come.

Shop Your Home

One of my favorite ways to change things up in my house is to go shopping—in my own home, that is. Because you can redecorate without spending a dime.

One of my favorite ways to keep things fresh and scratch that itch to change things up around the house came to me via my very wise mother. When I was growing up, I'd often come from school and walk into the house a bit confused. Everything looked different. The furniture may have been in a different arrangement, or there would be a plant or mirror in a new place. But she wasn't spending money on new home décor or furniture items. She was simply moving things around that we already had, repurposing them in different rooms in the house, or even just a different location within the same room.

It's easy, it costs absolutely nothing, and it doesn't require a trip to the store or buyer's remorse when the item doesn't fit in with your existing things. And it keeps things minimal—no additional bins of home décor items littering your storage room, or bags of items that didn't work sitting around and waiting to be returned. It always gives me the refreshed feeling I was looking for when my home décor feels a bit stale, and it breathes new life and appreciation into the things I already own.

Just Because It's Free Doesn't Mean It's for Me

I grew up in a family that frequently exchanged furniture and home goods between households as we grew up. It was pretty normal for my aunts and uncles to trade baby items, furniture, and even clothing with each other as their kids outgrew things. By passing those items on to me and my siblings, my mom and dad received items for free that they would have otherwise had to purchase for us.

As I've grown up and had children of my own, my siblings and I have continued that tradition. It's been incredibly helpful when it comes to providing what we need for our kids as they grow without having to spend the money to buy those items new. And it's given those items a second life, allowing them to provide more use to another family rather than simply being stored away unused or sent off to a donation center.

But I've also learned one important lesson through this: Just because it's free doesn't mean it's for me.

I am extremely appreciative that I'm fortunate enough to have these necessary items available without cost. But it's also incredibly easy to accept things simply because they're free. "Just in case." For years, I'd take things off my siblings' or parents' hands, carrying them down to the basement with the hope that they'd eventually get used. Take a wild guess at how many actually did; maybe one or two? The rest sat in storage collecting dust until I finally admitted to myself that I'd accepted the item and brought it into my home simply because it was free.

I'm pretty sure we've all done this at one time or another. It's human nature to accept free items—I mean, why not? It's free. But oftentimes, a free item appeals to us for only one reason: It isn't costing us a dime. Its appeal comes from the fact that we don't have to pay for it. And even if it means it'll simply gather dust in our already-crowded cabinets, closets, or storage rooms and spaces, we hold onto it because it would be wasteful if we didn't. Right? Except it's still wasteful. It may be sitting in our home rather than a donation center's shelves or a landfill, but if it's not being used, it's simply being stored in a more valuable location: our home.

This is true of the free couch that, although well-loved, has no place in your home, but you can't stand to pass up a free piece of furniture. Or it could be that bin of kids' clothing that sits in your closet because you've already purchased a closetful of items your kids love and wear, or that side table that you may possibly use someday when you rearrange your living room. Instead of finding a home where they will immediately be used and loved, these things are simply sitting in storage, collecting dust.

The next time someone offers you something for free, stop and think: Do I need this? Will I use this? Or will it simply sit in storage in my home? It all comes back to consuming intentionally. Sure, it's free. But if you're not absolutely certain that it'll be useful or appreciated in your home, just say no. There are plenty of people out in the world who would find more use for that thing. Pass it up and move on, and take pride in knowing that you held important space in your home for items that provide more usefulness and value to you. It can feel like a big deal to say no to those free things, but it's such an important component of simple living. The more often you practice saying no, the easier it gets, I promise.

THE DECISION FATIGUE DILEMMA

Decision fatigue is a real thing that moms are faced with daily. Our modern-day world offers up countless options to choose from on almost every decision we make. There's a freedom in having so many choices, but there's a huge burden that comes along with it, too.

It's called decision fatigue. Let's pretend that your brain is a big bucket of water. Each day, each decision you are required to make means removing a drop from the bucket. A bucket holds many drops of water; at a quick glance, it may not seem like you'd even make a dent in that bucket of water during the course of a day. But they add up—quickly.

Between the time your eyes open in the morning and the time you get the kids out the door for school, I bet you've made over one hundred decisions. Should I hit the snooze button or get out of bed? Should I brush my teeth now or after breakfast? It's cold—should I turn the heat up or throw on a sweatshirt? What coffee should I make? What cereal should I eat? What shirt should I wear today? Do I need a coat? If so, what type of coat?

I think you're catching my drift. Life requires us as parents to make so many decisions every single day—for ourselves, our partners, and our children. And each child multiplies those decisions. I have four children, so multiply that by four. It's enough to make your head spin.

Although each of those decisions may only require a second of your time, it adds up. With a plethora of available options for many of those choices, the energy consumed just in deciding one simple issue—like which shirt to wear in a closetful of shirts—can really pull on you. And each drop of energy that's drained with unnecessary or overwhelming decisions is one less drop of energy you hold onto to use in a more productive, enjoyable way.

Does that change the way you look at decision fatigue? It gives me a headache just thinking about it.

So what do you do? Eliminate the drain by decreasing the number of decisions and choices that you need to make. The less stuff you have, the less decisions you have to make—which is why it helps to have less stuff. If you only have three types of cereal to choose from, that's a much easier choice for you (or your children) to make at breakfast. Just five tops—all ones you love to wear—in your closet? Picking out an outfit for the day becomes so much easier.

Is this all starting to make sense? Sure, having choices is an amazing thing. But it can also be crippling when the number of decisions you are required to make is compounded daily. I'd prefer to have less options; fewer choices to make, and more energy back in my pocket to spend on the things that matter most to me. It's impossible to eliminate all the tough decisions we must make every day as parents, but by limiting the amount of energy we expend on decisions and concentrating it on the ones that truly matter to us, we can streamline our mental efforts and clear the clutter in our brains. And a less cluttered mind feels absolutely wonderful.

INTENTIONAL CONSUMPTION

Shopping with intention and limiting your consumption is an essential part of maintaining a decluttered, minimal home. But we still have to consume things. Many things sustain our homes and our families, and they need to be acquired. But there's still ways to alter those consumption habits and ensure we're purchasing with intention. Let's tackle one of the most essential, important types of shopping that you have to do even when you're pursuing a more minimal life: groceries. 'Cause we all have to eat.

Simplifying things requires a tiny bit of thinking and planning, and grocery shopping is no exception. When you are grocery shopping with a plan and a system, it should be a lot easier, but that doesn't mean it's effortless. There are still so many decisions to make when it comes to the items you buy to feed your family. As a mom, I'm sure you're well aware of the intense guilt that often comes along with the groceries you purchase. And there are so many options: organic versus conventional; whole foods versus packaged or processed foods; grocery shopping in person versus home delivery; and whether to buy in bulk quantities or purchase just what you presently need. It's enough to make your head spin!

Mental and emotional clutter are just as draining as physical clutter, and burdensome guilt around trying to do everything perfectly is a huge weight most mothers carry. I'm here to remind you that *doing the best you can* is enough. Do your research; purchase healthy options when you can. But don't let the ability to research and analyze everything to an excessive degree exhaust you when it comes to the food you feed yourself and your family. Let's jump into a few hot topic areas—I'll let you know how I simplify planning and thinking about these issues to just do the best I can.

Organic Versus Conventional

Before we dive in, let's make one thing clear: I am all for making the best and healthiest decision. I think most moms *are* doing the very best they can. With the access we have to social media and the internet these days, it's amazing how much information we can find with a simple search. It's an incredible tool and resource, but it can also be a huge drain on your time and energy. It's easy to become overwhelmed with all the information on even the smallest decisions, like whether to buy an organic or conventional item at the grocery store. And while I fully encourage you to do research and make decisions from an informed position as a consumer, I also believe that it's impossible to be fully educated on everything under the sun or to make perfect decisions 100 percent of the time.

Organic versus conventional food is one area where I find it easy to get drained. In an ideal world, of course we'd all want to feed our families the healthiest foods possible. But even on an abundant salary, the cost difference is exorbitant. I'm here to give you permission to make the best decision you can given your time and budget and to move on.

If the organic strawberries are three dollars more than the conventional ones and your kids plow through a carton in one sitting like mine, maybe it's not worth it to add that burden to your budget. If you end up not purchasing healthy, whole foods 100 percent of the time because your kids prefer the classic goldfish crackers over the organic cheese bunnies, buy the ones that will get eaten. Your preference may be to spend the bulk of your budget on an entirely whole-foods based, organic, gluten-free diet. Maybe you're struggling to make ends meet and you're buying more inexpensive, shelf-stable, processed foods. Or maybe, like most of us, you fall somewhere in between the two. Guess what?

We're all good moms—end of story. Make the decision, feed your family, and move on with your life. There will be another chance next week to make different decisions. Don't get so caught up in purchasing perfectly that you drain yourself (and your budget).

There's a lot of life to be lived out there, and the stress and burden of choosing perfectly is probably doing more harm to your mind and body than a bag of potato chips. Buy the potato chips. Eat the potato chips. Move on.

Online Ordering

I love taking a leisurely, kid-free walk in the aisles of my local grocery store. It's a simple pleasure, but it's not my reality these days—and I'm guessing if you're a mom of young kids, it's probably not yours, either. The reality looks more like rushed laps down the aisles, beelining to the essentials on my list while one kid runs ahead and pulls things off the shelves, one sits in the seat dropping Cheerios every three feet, and another has a meltdown when I refuse to add the ice cream to the cart. It's fun, right?

I'm here to tell you there's a better way to shop that will save your time and sanity and help you stick to your meal plan and budget: grocery pickup or delivery. Whether it's a free order pickup from your local grocery store, a prepaid order through a third-party grocery delivery service, or an online order with free delivery that requires a few dollars' tip, I'm here to tell you that the cost is probably worth it. Here's why.

Sticking to the List

Whether you're picking up in person or having it delivered, ordering your groceries online helps you stick to the list. If, like me, you're limited on self-control when it comes to in-store shopping (hello, impulse buys!), online ordering removes the temptation of aisle upon aisle of attractive displays and marketing and forces me to focus only on the things I truly need. It's also an easy way to avoid the inevitable meltdowns that happen when you take your kids to the grocery store—there's no arguing over adding items to the cart. Does anyone enjoy those dramatic affairs where you end up sweating and red-faced, doing your best to calm an irrational toddler while strangers stare and judge you? Me neither. Avoiding that is reason enough for me.

Saves Time and Energy

If avoiding toddler meltdowns isn't enough to sway you, ordering your groceries online also saves you a ton of time and energy. By following a list, it's easy to search, click add to cart, and be done. Instead of spending at least an hour each week buckling the kids into the car, corralling them into a cart and down the aisles, physically adding items to said cart, and then checking out, loading the car, and buckling four kids back into their seats, I can simply plop on the couch, pull out my phone, and have grocery shopping done in a matter of minutes. That's at least an hour added back into my day *every single week*. I'll take that trade-off of paying a few dollars delivery fee or delivery tip anytime. But that may not be worth it to you, and that's okay too. Again, what's your time worth? You decide.

Keeps You on Budget

Perhaps most importantly, online shopping has kept me on budget far more than any other tip, trick or strategy. By having the ability to watch my total add up as I add things to my virtual cart, I'm able to easily remove items if I'm over budget, or swap in less expensive versions of the same item instead of having to wait until I'm in the checkout line to embarrassedly ask the clerk to set items aside (trust me, I've been there). This may not be a big deal for you—maybe you walk through and add up item costs on a calculator. Or you're regimented enough that you've got price spreadsheets and a tally done before you even grocery shop. Maybe you have a ton of impulse control and are never swayed by an in-store sale or deal. Me? Not so much. So I stick to the simplest, easiest way and use online ordering to make sure I stay on budget. It's been an amazing tool as a busy mom, and if you haven't tried it out yet, I suggest you give it a whirl. Maybe you realize the cost isn't worth it. Maybe you realize you just prefer shopping in-store more. Or maybe it becomes your new best-kept secret for a weekly task you'll be doing for the rest of your life.

Buying in Bulk

One last hot topic when it comes to grocery shopping centers on how—and where—you shop. Small local shops? Large chain grocery stores? Wholesale stores? It's enough to make your head spin—as well as require you to make multiple trips a week to get the best of it all.

Buying in bulk is a huge asset when you've got a large family, but it's not for everyone. It may be a cost-saver even for a smaller family, but it's about being strategic and making sure it's a true benefit rather than just the lure of saving a few bucks. How many times have I bought an economy-sized box of some new snack food, only to have it expire before it's eaten? The answer is too many times to count. To be honest, bulk shopping is a large part of why I ended up in debt early on in my motherhood journey. I thought because I was saving money by buying more, I was saving money. In reality, I was just *spending* more money on things I didn't need and ended up doing the opposite.

A SIMPLER MOTHERHOOD

Wholesale club memberships and larger size bulk purchases will only benefit you if you *actually use* the items you're buying. Even though many stores sell a variety of shelf-stable goods, unless they're individually packaged, the clock starts ticking the minute you open that economy-sized jar of mixed nuts. If you don't eat nuts daily, they're probably going to go stale before you make it to the bottom of that container. I totally understand the draw of buying more at one time to save some money. But make sure you do some deep thinking before your next trip and start purchasing only the items that your family regularly consumes. You'll save yourself not only money, but also that awful buyer's remorse that creeps in when something you thought was such a deal ends up going to waste.

— — —

Again, I'm no rocket scientist. None of these concepts are brand-new, novel ideas—they're out there everywhere, being discussed in books, on forums, and in blogs around the world. But they make a huge difference when you're after a less complicated life. I'm here to share with you the things that I've tested and found to be tried-and-true ways to simplify how you function on the daily. They work well for me and my family, but that doesn't always mean they'll be a surefire solution for you. Try them out. See if they help. Tweak and customize them if there's some substance there, and ditch them if they just don't jive with the way your family lives. That's the beauty of life: having the ability to change and adapt things to work best for you.

CHAPTER 7

A Simpler Home

One of the biggest components of my job as a mom—and especially as one who stays at home full-time—involves all those thousands of to-dos, big and small, that keep our home running smoothly. It's a lot. All the things that are required to keep our family happy add up quickly and can easily overwhelm even the most organized and structured mother. I've been there—deep in that wearisome cycle of cleaning, tidying, and maintaining the same things over and over again.

But it's my job, one that I'm privileged to have. And I love that role a lot more these days because I've chosen to find ways to make it simpler. I've accepted the imperfect in my home; the monotony that often comes with raising children; and the mundane nature of many of the tasks that are required of me. And I've embraced that although I may have a ton of things to do, they're things I *get* to do, not things I *have* to do. Because guess what? A simpler home isn't going to miraculously remove all those chores, but it certainly makes things easier. And I'm about to share my favorite ways to do that. Easy is right up my alley when it comes to maintaining my home—and I'm betting you feel the same way.

LESS...BUT BETTER

Multitasking will ruin your motherhood.

I know it's a bold statement, but hear me out. For years, I searched endlessly for time-saving hacks, tricks, and tips to make my days more efficient. I bought into the daily message sold to us as women that we can do everything and be everywhere. And I know you've seen it, heard it, and felt it, too.

"We can do it!"

"Lean in."

"You can have it all!"

Guess what? You can. But it's just not worth it. Sure, you can absolutely find ways to maximize your multitasking and get it all done. Sure, you can have a career, a side hustle, a tidy home, and your own identity *and* be an amazing mother. And yes, it's absolutely helpful to work smarter, not harder—to get things completed more easily and efficiently; but not just simply for the sake of getting more done.

Productivity is not a measure of worth. Efficiency is amazing when it helps you accomplish what's necessary and creates more time and space in your life for the good stuff. But it's absolutely crippling when it's used as a weapon to leverage maximizing task accomplishment as the measure of a successful day.

Even if you are able to squeeze the most out of your day, something always has to give. And do you know what that something is? It's your ability to show up and enjoy any of those million moments you're being blessed with as a mother. In the grip of that constant desire to attain everything, get it all done, and maximize your productivity, you end up missing what's happening right now. In your quest to be everything to everyone, you empty your cup and end up completely drained and burnt out, with nothing to show for it but a completed to-do list.

So how about we all stop trying to do more, and start doing a little less? Less...but better, because your motherhood is so much more than a running list of accomplishments. Treat it like the gift it is, because your life is right here in front of you, waiting for you to show up for it. Make the courageous choice to honor and respect it by prioritizing the things that matter most to you, and stop striving to be that multitasking miracle that the world so badly wants you to be.

You may not get as many tasks done in your days, but I promise, you'll be getting far more life out of them.

Clean When You Can

For years, I tried out everyone else's cleaning routines, home maintenance schedules, and advice for how to structure my day as a stay-at-home mom. Guess what doing it that way provided: an endless feeling of failure when I didn't stick with the routine or schedule.

Now, I'm not saying you need to ditch a routine or schedule for maintaining your home if that works for you. Do you love having a checklist and knowing what needs to be done when? Awesome. Go for it! But if it isn't working for you, it's time to let it go.

As I mentioned, I spent years trying countless different structured routines, keeping different weekly, monthly, and daily to-do lists, and attempting to measure my worth by the tasks I accomplished. I was very productive, but I was also left with not much to show for it other than a heaping serving of resentment and bitterness. I wanted to do things on *my* schedule. Sure, I wanted to make sure our house stayed clean and organized. But some days, life got hectic. Kids got sick. Toddlers didn't nap. We wanted to go to the zoo...but it was "floors" day, and I had to get that done first. It was mentally and emotionally defeating to say no to those scheduled chores, just to have them loom over me as an incomplete task.

Sound familiar? If you're like me (and from the many moms I've talked to, I know there's a lot of you out there), I'm here to tell you it's okay not to have a checklist, a schedule, a routine, a to-do list. And even if you do have them, it's okay to say no if you don't have the time or energy to do those tasks (or just plain don't feel like it).

I'm also here to tell you that the minute you remove the daily, weekly, or monthly "have-to-do's" from your life, you're most likely going to enjoy doing all those things a little bit more. It's just science—and human nature. We're programmed to feel burdened and constrained the minute we're told we *have* to do something. But the minute it becomes a conscious choice? The minute we decide to tackle it because we feel like it? It just feels better. When we take ownership over our decisions about how to expend our time and energy, it just feels good.

While we're talking about getting things done, I'm also here to remind you that your worth is not measured by the number of tasks you accomplish in a day. Whether you're a stay-at-home mom, a working mom, or not a mom at all—we are all human beings who possess a ton of value, whether we get things done or not. Your worth is exactly the same whether you scrubbed the house from top to bottom or just laid on the couch and watched

Netflix—whether you changed the world as a CEO or wiped butts and did laundry.

Me? I'm a homemaker, a housewife, a stay-at-home mom—"unemployed." Whatever you want to call it, it's my job. And a big part of that job is maintaining my home. Let's be honest—cleaning the toilet does not bring me joy. Organizing our playroom toys for the 567th time isn't always an enjoyable experience. Mopping sticky floors and folding yet another load of laundry isn't top on my list of things I love doing.

But guess what? I'm grateful for that job. My husband and I worked hard for this house. We worked hard for these children. We worked hard so I could stay at home and raise our family, and we sure as heck worked hard for this life we've been blessed to create. We kept striving through hardships, losses, disappointments, and failures to make our dreams of raising our family in this way and in this home possible.

I clean when it's needed. I cook when it's requested. I organize and declutter and straighten up when our home needs more simplicity; more peace; more order. I don't follow schedules to check off a box on a list, or to have a completely clean and organized home, or to impress other people looking in on my life. I do it because I love making this house a home for us all. It may sound cheesy, and there are days when I swear profusely under my breath as I clean up another spill, wash another stained shirt, fix another broken toy. But then I check myself. I'm not going to do it with love all the time. But as long as I remind myself of the reasons why I'm doing what I'm doing, it becomes a lot less of a *have to do* and much more of a *want to do*. And no cleaning schedule or routine can make that happen.

Own Your Tasks

You are the one who gets to decide what you do. I'm tired of this narrative that as adults, we are required to do things we don't love. It's crap, if you ask me, because it's all about your perspective. Sure, I don't love mopping floors. Do you know why I do it? Because I have a mop I don't mind using, and I clean the floors when I want to—not when some weekly routine tells me it's the day; and because I've figured out that if I throw in a few drops of essential oils, crank up the jams, and bust it out when I'm well and ready, I don't feel like I'm doing something I don't want to do anymore. Perspective—it's a game-changer.

Sure, messes aren't joyful. I don't look at piles of dirty laundry or a playroom floor littered with toys and light up—and I'm sure you don't, either. But because I'm no longer overwhelmed by excess stuff (and the excess emotions that come with it), I'm much more likely to approach those messes with a little more grace and gratitude. Because I only hold onto what I need, what I love, and what I use (both for me and my family), the daily mess is less. That makes it much more manageable—in my time and energy output, as well as in my head. I don't spend hours dreading chores or the end-of-the-day pickup because I know it's no longer a mountain of things, and because it's all stuff that's been used or appreciated during the day, not just things that got pulled off shelves and discarded. (Ahem, I'm talking to you, prior me who bought her kids every toy they asked for and then watched as they literally pulled bins off the shelves, dumped them, and then didn't play with one darn thing.)

Now, I know you're probably thinking, "Emily, I didn't buy (or borrow) this book to have you lecture me on changing my attitude." Uh, yeah. I know. You're searching for the next mind-blowing rhythm or routine that will magically simplify your role. So I guess I'll give the people what they want. But full disclosure: I can't promise miracles. And as I've said so many, many times before, what works for me may (but most likely won't) be the magical answer you're searching for. But I'll share it anyway, because sharing is caring.

You've been warned. Here we go.

I mentioned earlier that I'm not a huge fan of planned or scheduled chores or routines, and I truly mean that. But there are some loose rhythms I operate on throughout my week that tend to stay fairly consistent, and they are as follows.

Laundry

I usually do laundry for our family of six every other day. Most weeks, that ends up being on Mondays, Wednesdays, and Fridays. I hate doing chores on the weekend, and I won't do it unless absolutely necessary, so this works out well for us.

It's enough laundry to fill our family hamper, which also happens to be the perfect size for one load of laundry. By the way, yes, we have only one hamper for the entire family. It lives in our hall linen closet, and it saves me so much time when it comes to picking up laundry and throwing it in the wash. Try it—you'll be amazed. No more jetting from room to room to gather everyone's laundry. It's life-changing.

Let's do some simple math, because your time holds immense value. I choose to do laundry three times a week for about twenty minutes a day. It takes me that amount of time to grab the hamper, throw a load in the wash, move it to the dryer, and then fold it. I let clean items pile up on our folding table throughout the week, then by choice, I put them away after Friday's load is folded—once a week. Because we do our laundry in the basement, it makes more logical sense: two trips, with two full baskets, once a week. It's just simpler. It takes less energy, and it saves me time.

It also forces me (and my kids and husband) to actually wear more of our clothing since our closets and drawers are only restocked once a week. Got a kid who would wear the same pink princess dress three times a week if it was clean? Yep, I've been there. This makes the decision simpler. It's not a fight against Mom anymore—it's a fight with the laundry. And amazingly, there's less whining when it's the washing machine's call.

Getting things done around the house shouldn't be awful. We aren't supposed to spend our lives being miserable about having to maintain our homes and things. We're supposed to figure out the quickest, most painless ways to accomplish the required things and then move on to the good stuff—because there's a heck a lot more of that kind of stuff if you make room for it.

Dishes

Our family goes through dishes quickly. Because my kids are young and my husband works from home, I'm preparing three meals a day for six people, not including snacks. (And let's get real, with kids, there are *always* snacks.) If I'm not careful, the sink will be full and the dishwasher will need to be run at least twice a day.

To keep things simple, I make sure each of my kids uses their own stainless steel thermos for their water. I also reuse their snack bowls throughout the day. This helps me limit the amount of new dirty dishes I do. For those mamas who need to hear this: Not every dish and utensil needs to be washed in the dishwasher. Did you eat a piece of toast for breakfast, and the plate has a few crumbs? Maybe try giving it a quick rinse and setting it aside for a later snack or meal rather than cluttering the dishwasher with a nearly-clean plate. By using our dishes intentionally, I'm able to run the dishwasher once a day most days, saving me valuable loading and unloading time.

And as mentioned earlier, to make this process even easier, I tend to let dishes pile up in the sink throughout the day, then add them to the dishwasher all at once. Rather than opening the dishwasher each time I have a few dirty dishes to add, I'm taking time to batch my efforts and load everything in there all at one time. By the end of the day, all the dishes are loaded. Hit run, let it clean overnight when we don't need access to any of the dishes from the day, and come morning, it's ready to unload while I brew my morning coffee.

It sounds simple—and it is. Doing this sets me up for a clean kitchen at night and an empty dishwasher and sink for the day, and it limits how much effort I spend on this necessity. By doing one task all at once (rather than several times throughout the day), not only do I dread it less, but I save my time and energy. Who wants to constantly have to think about loading a dishwasher? Not me. Maybe you enjoy a completely clean and empty sink throughout the day, so taking those extra minutes is worth it to you. Then that's your dish rhythm, and that's what you should stick to. Whatever it is, embrace the loose methods that work best for your family. It sure beats trying to fit yourself into someone else's mold.

Chores

I touched on this briefly earlier, but it bears repeating: You can't do *all* the things, *all* the time. Listen, some days, I want to clear my entire to-do list and draw a line through what's done just as much as the next woman. It's hard not to measure your productivity for the day based on the items crossed off your list. And some days, I amaze even myself at the number of tasks I'm able to tackle. But most days, I remember that motherhood is infinitely more enjoyable when I leave space in my schedule—for fun, for play, and for actually living my life.

So how do I make sure I get the most important things done without spiraling into a black hole of cleaning and organizing? I write it all down, and then I pick three each day.

Every week, I find a few minutes to grab my planner (since I'm a total physical, pen-to-paper planner kind of girl) and sit with my coffee—or a glass of wine. I then take five or ten minutes to write down everything that I want (or need) to accomplish for the next week.

I'm not going to lie—sometimes, I become a little overzealous and that list is entirely too overwhelming. But I tackle it, a few tasks at a time. I'll prioritize things based on time sensitivity or need and pick three things every day that need to get done. Some days, those three things are big things: laundry, cleaning bathrooms, grocery ordering or pickup. Some days, they're tiny: wipe down the countertops, put the laundry away, or take some donations for drop-off. I plan my week a day at a time, and it's all so manageable. Most days, I accomplish all three tasks before lunchtime. It feels good, but it's realistic—I'm not expecting too much of myself or setting myself up to fail. And once those items are done, I can choose to tackle more if I've got the time and energy. Or more often than not, I call it a day—feeling accomplished, on top of things, and with plenty of room in my day to really *live* my life—in whatever way I want.

Toys

I pick up our playroom once a day, at the end of the day. That's it.

I totally used to be that mom who cleaned up behind my kids. I was the mom who'd end up picking up the same baskets of toys five times a day—the mom who couldn't settle in with her kids and play unless everything was tidied. I couldn't handle the visual clutter. My own high standards for myself were projected onto my kids, and I couldn't accept the fact that they didn't care as much about a clean, tidy room as I did. I bet yours don't, either— because they're more focused on actually living their lives than on keeping things tidy. And shouldn't we be, too?

I know it is so nice to have a clean space, an organized toy system, a decluttered pantry. I know firsthand the therapeutic vibes that come from opening a perfectly organized medicine cabinet. But don't get so caught up in making (and keeping) things perfect that you forget to make it manageable, realistic, and livable. Because the calm doesn't reside in a perfect space—it resides in knowing that your home is lived in and loved on. Sure, it's organized, minimized, and easier to get back to normal. But real peace lies in letting go of that constant need for a put-together, perfectly tidied home. Because you live there. You have precious children that you're raising under that roof.

Our home exists in a less-than-perfect, lived-in state for much of the day now. And that's okay. I let the kids wreck the playroom most days. Many times, it spills over into our kitchen, the dining room, and seemingly every single inch of floor space in our home. And it's hard to let it go. But it's even harder to keep cleaning it up.

So I wait until the end of the evening. We crank the tunes, we all pitch in, and we put it all away. It eliminates the nagging and the projected expectations, and it fosters a whole lot more play, creativity, and fun. It's taken a lot of time and restraint, and even more practice. There have been lots of failures and plenty of times when I've regretted raising my voice in frustration over a playroom full of life. But it's worth it nonetheless. Because those messes they make? They're signs of life—signs of imagination, adventure, and exploration. And I don't want to stifle all that wonderful stuff for the sake of an orderly playroom.

Don't get so caught up in the everyday messes that you forget to find the magic in them. Motherhood is so, so messy—but it's also full of so many beautiful moments, too. And often, you've got to look past those piles of toys to find it. But it's there, just the same.

Reset Before You Rest

Along those lines, I treat the rest of my home in the same manner: We pick up the clutter at the end of the day. I know—some nights, I just don't have it in me to run around and pick up the stray dishes, the throw blankets and pillows from building forts, the shoes sprawled by the front door. But I'm always happier when I do. By doing a quick ten-minute walkthrough and resetting our home each evening, I wake up much more relaxed. I can start my day with a blank slate, and I'm not walking into a kitchen with cluttered countertops or stepping over piles of shoes on the floor on my way to make coffee.

Because we live in a two-story home, I keep a small woven basket at the bottom of our stairs to make this process even easier. Anything that needs to go upstairs to our bedrooms gets tossed in the basket as I clean up, and then I simply grab it to carry those items upstairs on the way to bath or bedtime. It keeps resetting the upstairs easier by making it one simple trip, and it also limits the clutter throughout the day. That unworn dress that needs to go back up to my daughter's room? It's tossed in the basket, and I move on with my day. That way, I'm not making trips up and down unnecessarily, which allows me to spend more time doing the things I want to do, rather than constantly picking up items from our living areas and carrying them up the stairs.

It took some time to settle into this routine, and there are nights I simply don't care enough to do it. So I let it go and tackle it in the morning when I have a bit more energy. But it's a rhythm that has made most mornings feel more peaceful, relaxed, and enjoyable. And most evenings, I easily tackle it because it's a manageable task. We have less stuff, so it's not so overwhelming, and each day, future morning me is thankful for the efforts of the evening reset.

You don't need to get rid of everything you own to be a minimalist. The way you feel about the items you own, the messes you make, and what it takes to maintain it all is just as essential as the items themselves. You probably won't feel as begrudgingly bitter hanging up those five freshly laundered tops that you love to wear and that feel great on pretty wooden hangers with room to breathe.

But if you have to shove twenty tops into an already full rack of rarely-worn clothing that either doesn't fit, isn't loved, or you don't even know how it got there, that's a totally different vibe.

If there's one thing you take away from this chapter, let it be this: Those messes are *blessings*.

That playroom floor covered in toys? The kids who created that mess probably starred in your hopes, wishes, and dreams for years—and now they're here in your life.

That pile of your partner's clothes in the corner of your bedroom floor is a reminder of the amazing person who decided they wanted to spend the rest of their life with you. And now they're here, sharing in every day.

That spilled dog food littering the kitchen floor is left over from the pup who rests loyally at your feet every morning, just happy to be able to spend their life quietly serving as a faithful companion through all of life's ups and downs.

Listen, I know it's not always easy to look at those messes this way. Some days, the frustration of cleaning up the same messes over and over can be overwhelming. The *Groundhog Day*-esque vibes of having the same mundane tasks to complete daily is enough to burden even the strongest, most grateful mother. Motherhood is often a monotonous, thankless job. But it's important work—quite possibly some of the most important work we can do in this lifetime. And every single one of us has a choice every single day to either live in how hard this stuff can be or to chase after joy.

I hope you make the right one.

CHAPTER 8

A Simpler Wardrobe

If you're here, I'm guessing it probably isn't. And you certainly aren't alone.

Getting dressed every morning used to be a constant battle for me: combing through way too many items, struggling to find the few that fit me and were comfortable and that I actually enjoyed wearing. It took up far too much of my time, made me feel bad about my body, and frustrated the heck out of me. Yet I went through this cycle over and over, every single day. Until I decided it had to stop.

My closet looks a lot different these days. My entire wardrobe—for all four crazy Ohio seasons—fits into a little over two feet of closet space: just a single hanging bar, a drawer system beneath it, and one storage bin for off-season items. And guess what? This is everything I need.

Sure, I'm probably not the most fashionable mom out there. I rock the yoga-pants-and-comfy-top look most days. But every single item in my closet is worn and loved. It takes me five seconds to pick out an outfit and get dressed every morning. It all fits me well and makes me feel good about my body, which can be pretty dang hard when you've been pregnant or postpartum for most of the last seven years of your life. And most importantly, it all makes me happy when I slip it on. It's comfortable, I know it fits well, and I can spend the rest of my day worrying about everything else but the clothes I'm wearing. Less clothing has literally rocked my world. Getting dressed every day is a pleasure now. It involves no stress or negative thinking, and most importantly, it requires absolutely no thought.

If you're eager to reclaim some time, order, and sanity in your days, it's essential to tackle your closet. It's just clothing. Literally—it's glorified pieces of fabric. So let's get started.

GATHER IT UP: ALL. OF. IT.

The first step to decluttering and simplifying your closet is to gather every item of clothing that you own. That means the closet and your dressers, but it also includes the coat closet, clothes storage bins, and everything from the laundry room, too. It's amazing how many items of clothing you'll find you own when you grab everything and collect it in one place—shoes, bathing suits, underwear, coats, all of it. This could mean clothing that's been stashed away because it's the wrong size, or maybe it's that bin of maternity clothing. Whatever it is, grab it. Because pulling it all out, gathering it together, and really examining what you have is such a critical step—one you absolutely must take if you want to be realistic about where you're at and where you want to be with your wardrobe goals.

I know, I know—it's going to make things take a little more time, and it's going to make a bigger mess before it gets cleaner, more streamlined, and simplified. But you need to be able to see everything you own so that you're able to clearly identify your best and most favorite things. For example, I'm a huge fan of neutrals, so it's easy for me to forget that even though I already have three basic black tees, I only really wear one of them. Gather everything so you can lay it all out and make the best decisions about your wardrobe.

When it comes to being able to really examine your clothing, I like to divide my items by category: tank tops, tees, blouses, sweaters, pants, shorts, pajamas, and so on. Once they're divided by general category, I like to subdivide them into smaller categories to make things even easier. For example, with my tank tops, I'll sort them into workout tank tops, casual tank tops, and dressy or date-night tank tops. Sorting them into subcategories helps because it gives me a clear indication of where I need to change my shopping habits. It's a lot easier to make decisions about your items when you can truly see what you have in each category. Again, dividing these items into piles can take a bit more time, but it makes the process of weeding through and sorting out your items infinitely easier.

When I pull everything out, not only am I able to see that I've got more than enough of my favorite staples, but viewing my whole wardrobe also helps me compare them. Those three black tees may be basic, but one is more comfortable and fits me better than the rest. But the other two? I bet I've been holding onto them just in case. They rarely get worn and instead just add clutter to my closet. Let's use that data for creating a wardrobe of our most favorite items and nothing else. That best-fitting black tee? That's the one I want to keep.

TRY IT ALL ON

Now's the fun (or not-so-fun) part. Try it all on. Every. Single. Item. Try on each one, even if you can't get it over your head or up past your knees. It may be a humbling few hours for sure, but it's essential to hammer home my point: I mean, if you can't even get it completely on your body, why is it taking up valuable real estate in your closet or your drawers? This technique may seem overly simple, but it's important to only keep what you love and wear hanging in your closet.

"But Emily, I'd have nothing left!" If you're in the thick of motherhood, I know you feel me on this one, big time. I've either been pregnant or within the first year of the postpartum stage for the entirety of my motherhood. And if I'm being realistic, I'm probably not going to fit into my pre-baby clothing anytime soon.

But for some crazy reason, I had a hard time letting go of those pretty little size small tops hanging in my closet. Season after season, all they did was take up valuable space, and I don't even really know why. Maybe I was hoping that seeing them there every day would motivate me to lose the weight. Maybe I was hoping it would prevent me from buying clothing in a bigger size. Whatever it was, it was only adding a burden to my life every single morning when I opened that closet.

I often have to remind myself that it's just fabric; it's completely replaceable, and it does not define me. Not only that, it's not serving me! Having a beautiful closetful of clothing that makes me feel bad about myself every time I go to get dressed? Not worth it to me. And it shouldn't be to you, either.

Once you've examined an item and tried it on, you're going to divide it into one of three categories: Keep, Store, and Let Go. Keep is simple—any item you love that fits well and that you wear often stays. Store is going to be the pile for your less-used but still loved and needed clothing items. Think special occasion dresses, or off-season clothing that may not fit in your closet, like coats. Let Go is going to be a grab bag of items: things you'll be donating or selling, or items too damaged to wear that may need to end up in the trash. Remember, the Let Go pile is always going to consist of items that can remain in your purgatory bin for as little or long as you like—consider it your emotional safety net. You don't have to send those items out your door immediately. The knowledge that you can always change your mind eliminates the anxiety and emotionality of putting many items in that pile. Trust your gut. If you don't love it...let it go.

What's left in your Keep pile should be only items you truly love and feel good wearing. It may be a smaller pile than you expected, but I guarantee you'll still feel a noticeable weight lifted from your shoulders. Why? Because what remains will be your most favorite, most comfortable clothing: the pieces that fit the body you're living in today, right now; the ones that feel good when you slip them on; the items that remind you that you're worthy of feeling and looking pretty, exactly as you are.

That feeling of worth matters because simple living isn't about perfect living. It's not about "arriving;" it's about rediscovering the joy in every single day of your journey in this life, flaws and all. And there's really no other category of stuff in your home that can help you find joy in yourself and embrace your imperfections more than a wardrobe full of clothing that allows you to feel good about your body just as you are right now.

PUT IT ALL BACK

Now comes the fun part: curating your wardrobe, however minimal it may be. Because after all that culling and weeding out, I bet you're not left with as many favorite items as you thought. Or maybe you're left with more than you realized. Either way, there's no magic number of items you need to retain. I think many people get stuck in this mentality of whittling their items down to a certain set number to qualify as minimal or simple. But I'm here to tell you, there's most definitely no set number. Minimalism and simple living look and feel different for absolutely everyone. You determine what works for you, whether that's more or fewer items than anyone else.

Also, with less clothing, you may find you no longer need as many pieces of furniture in your bedroom anymore. Personally, I love storing all my clothing in one place: the closet. I wouldn't have been able to do this years ago because I thought I needed hundreds of clothing items. In my twenties, even the walk-in closet was crowded. The thought of that seems absolutely absurd to me these days.

When I started pursuing simpler living, clothing was one of the first things I tackled. We had so much clothing in our home—bins of unworn items collecting dust in storage; dressers stuffed full of wrinkled, unloved items; and closet rods crammed with clothing, making it a project to remove the five tops I wore on repeat every single week. The reality of it all was that we were simply storing a whole lot of clothing we didn't wear or love. And yet, there it was, taking up so much extra space in our home, "just in case."

When we finally purged our clothing and narrowed our wardrobes down to only our most favorite items, we were left with half-empty drawers and closets; so I made the decision to move what we had left in our oversized bedroom dresser and use some secondhand drawers to store all our folded clothing in our closet. Not only did it free up valuable square footage in our actual bedroom, but it also made life significantly easier. Our entire wardrobes—hanging items, folded shirts and sweaters, bottoms, pajamas, socks, and undergarments—all live in our closet. This means that I can see everything I have at the same time, allowing me to grab a complete outfit in no time.

And that's just the system that works for me. You may need a different storage system. The system you should go with is the one that works for you. You may need to play around with a few different ones. With a smaller, simpler wardrobe, it's going to take some time to adjust your spaces and the systems you use to store those items. Experiment, and find the one that fits best.

ADDRESS THOSE BODY ISSUES

Now that you've streamlined your wardrobe, you're left with the items that fit you and make you feel best in your body and you've gotten rid of the rest. Great! You probably feel a little lighter with a less stuffed dresser or closet. But there may still be a bit of heaviness around all of that. This could be because although a minimal wardrobe will serve you well, it's not going to change your life, nor automatically make you fall in love with your body. And I'd be careless if I didn't pause the decluttering and simplifying chat to address what's most likely one of the biggest issues we as women face: finding peace with our own bodies.

I'll be honest: Last year was the first time I purchased shorts in the right size; not the size I wanted to be, nor the size I used to be, nor the size I'd be if I just lost a few more pounds. I bought the size that fit me in that season of my life—exactly and imperfectly as I was.

I bought myself shorts that didn't shame me into wanting to work out more, or envelop me in feelings of self-loathing each time I pulled them out of my drawer and slipped them over my generous thighs. Instead, they allowed me to move my body in all the ways it needed to move.

They were the size that permitted me to sit and tie my toddler's shoes without uncomfortably digging into the extra ten pounds that were hanging out on my tummy, a size that allowed me to focus on the million other more important things in my life than the dimensions of my hips, like chasing my kids around the yard and gleefully jumping through chilly sprinklers on a hot afternoon without pulling too-tight leg seams back down on my thighs. These right-sized shorts allowed me to tackle the daily to-dos in my home without stopping to adjust a too-tight waistband from pinching at my love handles. They let me cuddle on the couch with my husband at the end of a long day without worrying about that extra roll of fat spilling out of the top and ruining the mood during our few hours of downtime together.

For years, I let a larger clothes size and all the negative baggage that came with it keep me from accepting my body's actual size and shape. I let a little tag on my clothing dictate how I felt about myself every single time I got dressed. I purchased clothing that felt tight, constricting, and downright uncomfortable in the delusional hope that I'd be shamed enough to become smaller.

I'm finally over all of that.

The size of your clothing does not define the size of your worth. In fact, neither the size nor condition of *anything* in your life defines you. If we all stopped living for how we think we should be, what we want to be, or who we used to be, we could spend a lot more time living fully as the women we are.

And that sounds like a lot more fun, if you ask me.

CURATE WITH INTENTION

Now that you've simplified your wardrobe, it's essential to move forward with intention. That closet or dresser may look fabulous now, but it's not going to remain that way if you aren't careful about what you add to your wardrobe moving forward.

Once you've pared things down, you're probably much more aware of what clothing is needed to complete your collection. And that's a fantastic thing, but making sure you aren't just adding quick-fix items to fill those holes is equally important. After all, you've lived without those items up until right now—you don't need to complete that wardrobe tomorrow. Take the time to try things on and really think through how they'll function for you and complement your wardrobe—it's absolutely essential. You worked hard to create this new, more simplified wardrobe, so don't rush to clutter it back up again. If you choose and purchase items that you need, that fit well, and that will be worn often, you won't have to go through this process all over again in a year.

The same steps work for everyone else in your home, too. You can follow this exact process for your kids and your partner when you're looking to simplify their wardrobes. It'll take time, but streamlining everyone's clothing will simplify things in so many ways. Think less whining, less morning chaos before school, and less laundry to do—these are reasons enough, am I right?

But please remember that these decisions are for them to dictate when it's their own clothes on the chopping block. You can't force someone else to view their things in the same light that you do. Your kids may enjoy having more items than what you would prefer they had—and that's totally fine. Your partner may have sentimental memories attached to their collection of college tees. That's okay, too! Move through this process as a team, and let them make the decisions as often as you can. It's essential for them to own their own journey to simplicity, too—however different it may be than your own. Remember: Simplifying looks different for every single one of us. Beautiful, right?

CHAPTER 9

Simpler Self-Care

Self-care: it's such a trendy term these days, especially in the motherhood community. And to be honest, it often gets a bad rap. But no one can argue that it's not important, just the same. There's a whole spectrum of self-care, and as women, we vary widely across the spectrum when it comes to what we need to do to take care of ourselves. Some mamas consider a luxurious day at the spa to be essential self-care. Others only need a long, hot shower to feel like they've taken time to recharge their batteries. But whatever your idea of what self-care looks like, it's an absolute necessity for a happy mother.

Raising children can drain your energy quickly because motherhood is often a one-sided cycle of giving. Children, especially younger ones, require a lot, and they often don't offer up much in return. They require all of your attention, love, and care, and when you multiply that by two, three, or even more, it adds up quickly. Taking care of yourself and making sure you're getting what's needed when it comes to the basics—sleep, nutrition, hydration, and downtime—is important. Make it a priority.

FILL YOUR CUP

Being a mom is hard work. It's exhausting on every single level— physical, mental, and emotional. And as with anything else in life, when the battery is drained, there's nothing left to give, which is why it is so important to recharge. You can't give to anyone if you aren't doing the things that help make you the most present, satisfied person you can be—as a mother, a wife, a friend, or a coworker. Today's society expects women to be able to do it all, and although that's a lofty aspiration, it's just not realistic without putting ourselves and our needs first.

Yes, those little people need us. But they also need us to be the best version of ourselves, too. So taking the time to prioritize your needs is the furthest thing from selfish. In fact, if you do so consistently, I think you'll find that you're able to give more to your family, which is as selfless as it gets. But knowing what fills your cup is often the hardest part. It's easy to get lost in our role as mothers and put ourselves on the back burner in the quest to master that role. That's why it's key to recognize when we've pushed ourselves too far and stretched ourselves too thin so that we can make a course correction.

This is the only body, the only mind, the only soul we'll have in this lifetime, yet we often push ourselves past our limits. We frequently run ourselves into the ground to keep a tidily organized home, a balanced budget, and a full fridge. We repeatedly saddle ourselves with an always-busy schedule, or an endless to-do list. But what about taking care of ourselves as mothers? It's an item on that list, way down at the very, very bottom, and we often only attend to it when we're done with the rest.

I get it; being a mother is important work. But do you know what's most important? *You.* Nothing—and I mean *nothing*—good comes from a burnt-out mom. No amount of coffee and motivational quotes can get you through it. Eventually, it will all come crashing down, one way or another. It always does.

Make sure you stop before that burnout hits. Make time for yourself. Find what helps remind you that you have your own identity outside of your role as a mother. The thing that fills your tank back up may be small, but it's *so* important. It could be a short walk in the neighborhood in silence to clear your head; shutting yourself in the pantry and snacking on chocolate without a needy toddler asking for a bite; or handing the baby off and heading to bed an hour early to catch up on sleep. Self-care isn't always a hot bubble bath, a spa pedicure, or a girl's weekend away (although those things may very well be exactly what's needed to bring you back to an even keel).

Chase after that debt-free life. Declutter every closet and drawer. Minimize your commitments, your to-do list, and all that clutter crowding your mind. Learn to live with less of all that stuff. But also, remember to just stop and pause. Because this is your life, right this very minute. It's being lived, whether you're fully there for it or not. It's happening whether your tank is topped off or you're riding on empty. It's your one beautiful, wonderful life. How you choose to feel on that ride is entirely up to you.

Don't get so caught up in getting things all simultaneously in order that you forget to enjoy the here and now. Don't put off resting and being present to listen to those giggles from your children until after you get all the laundry done. Don't wait to buy those lovely tulips or that deliciously hot cup of coffee until you are completely debt free. Don't prioritize the house becoming perfectly tidy and clean over sitting down, looking out the window, and appreciating that glorious morning sunshine. Don't hold out for an unscheduled weekend to sit down and crack that really good book.

Don't wait.

Because there will always be something in life pulling at you, screaming in your ear that it's important and needs your attention. There will always be another item on your to-do list to tackle, another mess to pick up, and another sticky floor to clean. And self-care isn't about having everything in order before you sit down and take care of yourself; it's not about pushing yourself to keep going on an empty tank before you take that break you so badly need. It's about making enough space in your head and your heart to be able to see through the ever-present clutter of life and set it aside so you can be present for something so much better.

For me, self-care is less about how I incorporate special moments into my weeks and more about how I choose to navigate through my days. Was it a rough night when the baby didn't sleep well? I'm taking every nonessential task off my plate and resting my body. Am I feeling emotionally exhausted from my toddler's tantrums? I'm asking my mom if she can spend some time with him for a few hours while I get a break. I understand that not everyone always has that luxury, but it's critical to identify when you have that option and take advantage of it. You don't *have* to do everything, all the time. Releasing that burden of expectation can often be enough to recharge your batteries. Just giving yourself permission to have a bad day—or an unproductive one—can be just as life-giving as any self-indulgent moment.

Today, I make sure I get the essentials whenever I can: a hot cup of coffee first thing in the morning, a proper breakfast, and most days, a shower all to myself. Doing this matters because I used to be really, really good at putting myself last, and it didn't serve me at all. I spent years not prioritizing these things. They inevitably got pushed aside, replaced by a microwave beeping with an already-cold-again mug in it, the leftover bites from my toddler's plate, a nice quick shake of dry shampoo on my hair, and a top knot. I told myself that everyone else's needs were more important. And somehow, I pushed my own needs further and further down on the must-do list (or worse, neglected them altogether).

In this season of motherhood, I'm making sure to find a way to balance both—to take care of my family and myself. By making that effort to either prioritize those needs or postpone them—but not ignore them, I'm creating my own form of daily self-care. Please, if there's one thing you do when it comes to your motherhood, it's making sure to prioritize yourself every single day, especially when it comes to the little things. Because what we need is often not some grand, day-long sabbatical from the kids, but maybe just five minutes of silence in the bathroom with the door closed so we can do our business in peace. It doesn't always have to be a big, planned event when it comes to prioritizing ourselves; but it often involves reaching out and asking for help.

LEARN TO ASK FOR HELP

You simply cannot be everything to everyone all the time. It's just not possible, and it's definitely not healthy. Whether it's your mental health that's on the line, a looming list of to-dos that you simply don't have the time to tackle, or even just a listening ear so you can air your feelings, it's important to learn to ask for help. And the sooner you learn to do that, the sooner being a mother will feel a bit less heavy. Ever heard the expression "It takes a village"? It's true to an epic degree. Motherhood is a tough job, and it's not one to be done alone. It takes friends, and family, and even strangers to help get through some of the toughest days. But it's not going to happen if you don't reach out and ask for support.

Have you ever seen someone drowning—like, actually drowning in a pool? It's scary. I was a lifeguard for years and witnessed it more than I would have ever wanted. It's terrifying...and it's mostly silent. It doesn't appear how you'd picture it; there's often no cry for help or obviously frantic splashing around. Most often, it's simply a person who's too tired or physically unable to stay above the waterline. They're exhausted; they're fighting to keep their head above water as they bob above and below the surface. It was my job as a lifeguard to stand watch and look for this, because no one else around the drowning person ever really noticed when it was actually happening.

But sadly, there aren't always lifeguards on duty when it comes to motherhood. It's often not noticeable to those around you when you're drowning in your role as a mother. Oftentimes, you slip under the surface and silently struggle, often right in the midst of those closest to you. And unless you reach out and ask for help, you might not get it. It's hard being vulnerable and admitting you can't do it all. I've been there, and I know what it's like to have to wave the white flag and admit I need help. But once I do, things become infinitely easier. Don't get so caught up in how you think others will view you that you refuse to get the help you need. Whether it's your husband helping with chores that desperately need doing, getting someone to watch the kids for half an hour so you can get out of the house for some quiet time, or even seeking out therapy when life seems too tough to handle on your own, know that there are always wonderful people in the world who are willing to be there to help you out.

Asking for help isn't a sign of weakness, it's a sign of strength. Being able to put aside your pride and ask for assistance so you can be a more functional person, both for yourself and for the people around you—that is the ultimate sign of self-awareness.

And there are folks out there everywhere who want to help, people who make their living and find intense gratification in extending their services and expertise to help you get to a better, more joyful place in your life. The helpers are there, you just have to take advantage of what they have to offer. As children, we're always taught to look for the helpers, and that shouldn't change as an adult. Seek out the friends, family, or even new acquaintances in your community and utilize the resources they offer. If such resources are not easily found in your community (since we're not all privileged enough to have a built-in village surrounding us), do some research and legwork and find them. They're out there, just waiting to help—I promise.

SIMPLIFY THAT SELF-CARE

One of the biggest perks of simpler living has been my discovery that when life feels easier, I don't need as much "extra" to get me back to a joyful place. This means that I end up needing fewer of those last-minute "I need a break" moments and can really enjoy my daily life. If you're living simply, life feels lighter—and that means even the tough days are a bit easier to endure. I like to think that if you're living right, you shouldn't need to escape your life to relax because you've already created a life that brings you joy and happiness. When you remove all the excess—things, people, and commitments—that don't serve you, you're left with a lot more room for things that do.

It feels counterintuitive: Less is more? How? And I get it—it feels that way because we're constantly told that adding more things into our life will make us happier, that if we're upset, sad, stressed, or lonely, there's a tangible item that will fix that and miraculously solve our problem. But remember that possessions are tools and nothing else. They deliver utility to our lives, and they may also look beautiful, but they won't fill a void, heal a broken heart, or remove stress from your life.

Clearing your space of all those unfulfilling items will make more room for the true emotions you're feeling to surface. This may bring true peace and joy to your life, or it may allow those negative things you've been hiding behind all your possessions to surface. Keep in mind that although this may be uncomfortable, it's an essential part of the process. Identifying what your true needs are with the clutter of your things removed will help you find ways to take care of yourself that will bring lasting change.

When the little things begin to bring you joy, you won't need so many of the big things. Stop waiting for tomorrow, next week, or next year to enjoy your life, because every day of your life is a celebration. Don't sacrifice your immediate happiness in your everyday life and delay your gratification for a bigger, better moment. When you stop living in anticipation and start living in the present, you'll squeeze so much more pleasure out of motherhood. And isn't that what life is about? None of us are promised tomorrow. Don't drive yourself into the ground and postpone your happiness in the hope of getting everything in order before you sit down and appreciate what you've already got. Every day we wake up is a gift. Make sure you're treating it that way. And if you are, I think you'll find those little moments in life will constantly recharge your batteries with small, energizing doses of renewal, offering up joy and gratitude in even the most mundane minutes of your days.

But also know that there will be days where there simply aren't opportunities to refill your cup, times in your life when you just can't seem to catch a break. That's okay—those are days when those self-care moments need to happen more than ever. Recognize and accept that those hard days, weeks, and months are just part of the seasons of motherhood, and know that taking care of yourself when you can will carry you through them.

And while you're making time and space for those things that fill your cup, please remember that self-care isn't selfish—it's self*less*. By taking care of yourself, you're making sure you're able to fully take care of the people you love the most. And you're worth it, too, because you sure as heck can't fill up anyone else's tank when you are running on empty.

CHAPTER 10

Simpler Seasons

Ah, the holidays. If you're anything like me, the thought of the holidays simultaneously brings up feelings of sheer excitement and pure chaos. Celebrating the seasons through the eyes of my children is quite possibly one of the most incredible experiences of my life, as well as one of the most hectic. Watching the joy and happiness they experience from the holidays with all of their magic is truly one of the best parts of motherhood. But such occasions can also bring a ton of stress with them. Between the financial burdens, the extra work needed to bring all those celebrations and events together, and the chaos of balancing your own experience with the happiness of your children and your family, it can be tough to find a happy medium.

But discovering that balance is key. I think that as mothers, we often get so caught up in making the holidays a magical experience for everyone else that we forget we're supposed to be celebrating and enjoying those moments as well. Simplifying life has made the holidays infinitely easier for me, and there are many ways to ditch the stress, pressures, and expectations that often come along with these occasions and instead prioritize the most joy-giving, important parts.

The little things *matter*.

Every season, you're going to be bombarded with newer, better, and more exciting ways to celebrate the season. As the holidays roll around, your feed is probably jam-packed with the cutest kids' activities, swoon-worthy front door décor, and Pinterest-perfect baked goods. And if you're up for the challenge and those things are meaningful to you, go for it! But don't feel guilty if you're seeking a less complicated holiday season for your home and your family. That's more than okay, too.

More isn't always better—in fact, it rarely is. We keep it simple in our home around the holidays by focusing on more of the little things, and I couldn't be happier about it. For example, every fall, my kiddos go nuts over our annual tradition of picking out a mini pumpkin for each of them to place by their beds. It's as cheap as can be, and it only takes thirty seconds to let them each pick one out and add them to my shopping cart while we're at the store. And it brings them such immense joy, I can't imagine not repeating it every year for the rest of their childhood.

I promise, one little pumpkin by their bed can bring as much joy as a home full of them.

Ready to make the seasons a little more fun, a lot less stressful, and a whole bunch simpler?

SEASONAL SINKING FUNDS

One of the most significant and stressful components of celebrating any holiday throughout the year is the financial burden that comes along with it. Sure, Christmas is an expensive holiday and therefore tends to be the most stressful one. But there's a cost associated with them all—from Easter candy to Fourth of July home décor, not to mention birthday gifts, party snacks, and favors. It all adds up quickly, and if you don't have a plan for your spending, you can easily stress yourself out.

The easiest solution I've found is to create a celebration sinking fund. To begin, add up all of what you've spent in the past year on anything related to a celebration or the holidays. Christmas gifts, Christmas decorations, and the like are part of this tally, sure. But it also includes costs that you probably haven't included in your accounting, like that annual Valentine's Day dinner, all those birthday cards and gifts, the groceries you purchase for your family Easter brunch, and the Christmas outfits you purchase for your kids every year. Trust me, you'll be amazed at how quickly all that incidental spending adds up, but it's essential to figure that out.

Once you've got that number, divide it by twelve. That's your monthly sinking fund savings figure: Every month, you need to take that amount of money and deposit it into your savings. As you spend on any celebratory items, take note of those purchases. At the end of the month, take the total amount of whatever you spent on those costs and move that money from your sinking fund back over to your checking account, or use it to pay that amount off your credit card if that's where the spending happened. What remains in the fund carries over to the next month, and so on through the year. By the time November rolls around and you're planning what usually ends up being your biggest holiday spending of the year, you should have left exactly what you need to spend on those major holiday purchases.

This works extremely well for most people based on the way the seasonal spending falls. By setting aside the overage throughout the months, you end up creating a little nest egg to spend on those larger purchases at the end of the year. No more stressing about how you're going to pay for Christmas; no more unpaid credit card bills that keep adding up with each small present, card, and birthday dinner you finance. You've got a built-in safety net for all those incidental purchases that are often hard to account for in your normal budget expenses. And more importantly, you save your sanity. You're not constantly stressing about how you're going to pay off that post-Christmas credit card bill, or struggling to make room in your food budget for those large grocery store purchases around Thanksgiving. It's a quick, easy way to plan for the future and make celebrating the seasons an easier, breezier thing, and I'm all about that.

SIMPLER DECORATING

Seasons and holidays used to be my excuse to redecorate our home and buy new stuff. I'd pick things up from Target, Home-Goods, Michaels, Hobby Lobby...you name the store, I was there, buying up all the cute new seasonal décor pieces for the holidays. I'd spend tons of money and clutter up every countertop and surface of our home, yet it still never felt quite right. It never looked like all the Pinterest pictures I'd pinned; in fact, it never felt anything but more crowded. I often couldn't even find good places in my home for half of those super-cute décor pieces.

At the end of the season or holiday, I'd have two or three large bins full of décor, and I'd need to find a place to store it for the next eleven months. Then the following year, I'd inevitably find new décor I wanted to buy—the new trend for the season. And the destructive buy-decorate-declutter cycle would continue.

Not anymore. Listen, I am all for some cute holiday pieces around the home. I enjoy the changing of the seasons here in the Midwest and love having items in my home that signal those changes. I'm not suggesting that you forego holiday décor altogether, but rather that you only hold onto things that evoke sentiment, bring you joy, and don't make the holiday season any harder than it already is.

Myself, I've pared my décor down so that each season now fits in one storage bin (with Christmas being the exception). And most of them aren't even full. I've found items that add to my home and make me happy—ones that welcome the seasons and remind me of the joy contained in each unique turning of the year. For me, that's just a handful of beautiful things; however, you may enjoy going all out with your home décor, and that's okay, too! Find your own balance, but only display items that bring you joy. Don't decorate for anyone else but yourself—it's *your* home, *you* live there. Fill it with things that make it your own happy place. Don't let the idea of keeping up with the Joneses infiltrate your most sacred seasons, because the holidays are meant to be experienced, not just staged. It's about finding that sweet spot when it comes to seasonal things that bring joy to your home and your heart without crowding, cluttering, and adding chaos to it.

What's the easiest way to figure out what seasonal décor items really add to the season for you? Let them sit in storage for a year. I challenge you to get your items out for each season or holiday as it comes. Then, utilize only the ones you love best. Leave the rest in storage, and live through that season with just the favorite items you selected. I'm willing to bet that you won't miss any of those extra things in storage. If you do, by all means—bring them out! Add them to your home and appreciate them. Or perhaps realize that the minute you've brought them out of storage and into your home, they're just adding clutter. Either way, you'll get the opportunity to find out what brings you joy and what you've been putting out just because it's in the Christmas bin. It'll save you time and money, and it will help you feel a little less burdened and cluttered in your own home during the holiday season. I think you'll find that you need a lot less "stuff" to get you in the holiday spirit than you previously thought.

SIMPLER GIVING

While we're talking about the holidays, gifts obviously play a huge role in our celebrations. Whether it's birthday gifts, Christmas gifts, or just a thank-you gift to your kid's teacher at the end of the school year, remember that it's the sentiment that matters, not the monetary value. I think we all often feel that the higher the cost, the more value the recipient will feel when that item is given. But then again, I think we've all also experienced that this is absolutely not the case. For example, I bet you spent your baby's first Christmas finding all the best baby toys to present to them. You probably spent way too much time and money researching, purchasing, and wrapping those items and then couldn't wait for their first Christmas morning. Yet after the gifts were presented and unwrapped, I guarantee that every single one of your babies enjoyed playing with the boxes or the wrapping paper more than the gifts themselves.

Am I making my point clear? Rather than focusing on their value from a financial perspective, I encourage you to start giving gifts with intention. Whether it's your child, a family member, or a friend, I'm betting that the gift they'll love the most is the one that comes from your heart. So go ahead and buy your children all the beautiful, well-made, neutrally painted wooden toys your heart desires. They'll make your playroom look fabulous, and perhaps your children will love playing with them. But if all they wanted was that singing, dancing Elmo doll, those wooden toys will serve solely as playroom décor—the kind that often clutters your playroom floor without actually being played with.

While we're talking about value, I also encourage you to give experiences over things whenever possible. It's not a new concept by any means, but if you're used to giving tangible gifts, you'll soon realize it takes a bit more planning and effort. Experiential gifts require really knowing a person; selecting the right ones takes *really* understanding their interests and taking time to give something they'll be happy to add to their lifelong treasury of memories. Sure, it's a lot quicker and easier to drop by Target and pick up a ten-dollar candle. But choosing an experience to give as a present doesn't have to be some lavish, intricate event. Possibilities include a card with an invitation to a lunch date, a gift card for their favorite nail salon, or a package of swim lessons, dance classes, or tickets to the amusement park nearby. It doesn't have to be expensive or involved, it just requires knowing a person's heart and what they enjoy doing in their lives.

When it comes to gift lists for your children so family members know what to get them, asking for experiences makes things easier. My children have *plenty* of toys, so instead of flatly declining gifts from relatives or friends, I simply ask for experiences. A day with his Nanna makes my six year old feel like he won the lottery. A spa day at home that includes painting my four-year-old's toenails is her definition of opulence. And each experience and all the happiness it brings lasts far longer than yet another toy left sitting in the corner after a day of play. It's certainly not that our kids don't ask for their share of tangible gifts, but when toys are requested, we try to focus on those that will provide the most open-ended play and spark the most creativity in their hearts. A science experiment kit, playdough, or art supplies keep our kiddos entertained far longer than a singing, dancing toy.

All that being said, minimalism doesn't mean never owning the occasional noisy, light-up toy. If it's something you know they love and will likely enjoy daily, give them the toy and move on. A simpler life isn't about doing everything perfectly—gifting included. And it follows the same rules as any other type of consumption in which you choose to partake. If it brings joy or beauty to the recipients' life, it's a worthwhile gift. After all, the heart of gift-giving isn't in the gift itself—it's in the thought behind it. Make that your priority, and things will become infinitely simpler.

SIMPLER CELEBRATING

What's the best part of the holidays? It's not the gifts, or the decorations, or even the seasonal music. (Anyone else love turning on the Christmas tunes *way* ahead of December 1? No? Just me?) Anyways, the best part of the holidays is really the celebration— spending time with your family and friends, making memories, passing down traditions, and reveling in the nostalgia and magic of it all. We all know that, and yet it's so easy to get caught up in the superficiality of the seasons: the gifts, the outfits, the Christmas card photos. Those are all amazing components of each year's important and exciting celebrations, but it's hard to avoid a whirlwind of chaos when it comes to annually recreating a Pinterest-perfect holiday.

Let those perfect images *go*. Get them out of your head. When it comes to celebrating, all they will do is pile unnecessary and unattainable standards onto your shoulders. Those expectations don't make the celebration any more fun. They don't earn you any extra wonderful memories. Instead, all they do is tax your finances, your time, and your energy. That doesn't sound like the warm, fuzzy feelings you want to associate with a birthday party, Christmas morning, or Thanksgiving family dinner, right?

The easiest way I've found to simplify the holidays is to prioritize what's most important for you and your family. That may mean saying no to holiday party invites or planning a smaller, less expensive but more thought-out birthday gift selection. It may mean buying cupcakes from the store rather than spending hours making them from scratch, or planning fewer Christmas family events and prioritizing the traditions that really matter and will be the most fun for your kids. Basically, it means learning to say no to any event or expenditure of your time and energy that isn't going to add a ton of value to your holiday experience, and learning to say yes to the things that will.

Quality over quantity—it really holds true here. Don't spend those special moments spreading yourself thin and running yourself ragged for the sake of the perfect photo op or the ideal party—it's just not worth it. That's not what's going to matter years from now when those kids are grown and out of the house and passing on traditions to their own children. What will matter is the times you were present with friends and family celebrating with you, the times you *really* soaked in those special moments and witnessed the magic of the season in all its glory. It's hard to say no, but it's absolutely worth it. Don't spend another holiday "getting through it." Be there, show up, and enjoy it. That's what holiday celebrations are really all about.

A SIMPLER MOTHERHOOD

SIMPLER STANDARDS

Let that holiday guilt *go*.

The seasons shouldn't just be a long list of to-do items and activities to cross off and accomplish. I know, the rest of the world tells you otherwise. At every holiday or change of season, there's a constant stream of gift guides flooding your feed. There are beautiful photos of perfectly decorated homes, perfectly crafted DIY projects, and all kinds of holiday activities for the kids, with every single post urging you to add things to your mental list of holiday musts.

Don't let it make you feel less-than if you're not doing all the things for each holiday season, because a simpler holiday isn't just about less gifts, less décor, or less spending—it's about a little less of *everything*. A simpler holiday means holding tight to the cherished traditions that you love and discarding the rest. And you better believe that includes mental and emotional baggage, too.

I'm willing to bet you have some form of holiday guilt burdening your heart each season. Maybe you decided to ditch the holiday cards last Christmas, or you're already dreading making next year's annual Thanksgiving Day dinner. Maybe you don't want to pack a million plastic eggs with candy and spend hours hiding (and then finding) them all over your yard. Or maybe you feel like your holiday décor doesn't hold a candle to all these perfectly decorated homes in your neighborhood every December. Perhaps you feel guilty for spending too much on birthday presents and spoiling your kids a little bit after an especially tough year. Or maybe you feel bad about the new plastic toys that will fill your home this winter, but those toys are all your kids have on their Christmas list for Santa so far.

Whatever it is weighing on your soul, let it go. Because a simpler holiday isn't just about less clutter in your home, it's about less clutter in your seasons, less clutter in your head, and most certainly less clutter in your heart. Guard against those expectations. Lower the bar. And remember, you are the gatekeeper to a simpler life during the holidays. You get to actively decide how your seasons look and feel.

Make sure they bring you—as well as the ones you love—joy.

CHAPTER 11

Simpler Storage

Hi, I'm Emily. I'm a minimalist, but I still have things in storage.

Yep, you read that right. And I'm betting that even if you lead a simpler life, you've still got a few things to store, too. The reality of life—especially as a mother—is that there will be many, many seasons that involve different needs, and those needs often require material things: Think baby bouncers, children's clothing, and even holiday décor. It's just not practical to assume we can always rent, borrow, or do without many items that are less used, but still practical. And although that's an admirable goal, I'm not about doing this minimalism thing *perfectly*, I'm about doing it *practically*.

So with that being said, let's figure out how we can store the extra, but in a simpler, more organized way.

HOW TO STORE

Everyone lives differently. Myself, I'm blessed to have ample closet space as well as a half-empty basement storage room. These areas are used to hold our seasonal items, clothing in sizes that aren't presently being worn, and many of the baby and toddler things that we cycle through as our kids reach different ages and stages in those first two years. You may be living in a tiny apartment with limited closet space, or a large house in the suburbs with a full basement to stow your less-used items. Whatever your circumstances, I encourage you to use the dimensions of the storage space you have as your limit when it comes to storing stuff.

Is your closet full? That's a sign that you need to get rid of some items if you want to bring new ones in. Basement impossible to walk through? It's probably time to host a yard sale, sell some things on Facebook Marketplace, or maybe just donate them to the nearest donation center. Because living within your means also means living within your home's limits. If you're in a smaller space, take it as a sign to both maximize the storage areas that you do have and more closely examine all the things that are taking up that valuable space.

This certainly doesn't mean storing things simply because you have the room to do so. If you're blessed to live in a large home with huge walk-in closets, that doesn't mean you have to fill them. And if your home seems "too small," maybe it's simply because you're storing too many things. Being able to recognize the situation you are in and adapt to it accordingly is key to simpler living, because you can't out-organize clutter. Sure, there are ways to get creative when it comes to keeping things simply stored. But the storage solutions and organizing products you're eyeing won't make things simpler for you if you're living in excess.

WHAT TO STORE

The typical items I mentioned earlier are popular items that we all have—think Christmas (or other holiday) lights and ornaments, off-season clothing, and keepsakes. They all need a place to go that's out of the way and doesn't impede your access to the things you use daily. But it's also equally critical to think outside the box and store less-used items, relocating them from your everyday spaces and freeing up valuable real estate in your closets, pantry, and bathroom vanities.

For example, my husband and I both come from big families. We have a lot of entertaining pieces, and we use them for most holidays and special occasions. But that doesn't mean they need to live in my kitchen or dining room—both small spaces. So we got creative and repurposed some old kitchen cabinets to create our own storage cabinets that reside in our rather large living room. They make use of what would otherwise be empty space, they hide all the clutter, and they store all our pieces. Oh, and our television and some lamps live on them. Doing it this way keeps the items accessible, but out of the way. Win-win, right?

Same thing goes for our seasonal linens. We live in the Midwest, so summers are hot and winters are cold. That means thick, cozy, down comforters in the winter and light quilts in the summer on all our beds. I could keep them in our tiny hall linen closet, taking up valuable real estate—or I could store them in a bin in our extra storage closet and simply access them twice a year when the seasons change. Easier, right?

This can be applied to so many other things. Your extra pantry items don't need to live in your pantry! Create a shelf in your basement and grab them as needed. Your extra shampoo and conditioners? You could choose to just buy them as they're used up—a novel concept, I know. Or if you enjoy stocking up on a deal and buying more than what you'll use at one time, store them in a basement rather than shoved into your bathroom vanity, cluttering it up. Then you won't need to dig past them every single time you're in search of a clean towel or extra roll of toilet paper!

It seems simple, but tuning up how you store things also requires a lot of creativity on your part. All our homes and our spaces are different, and they each function differently for us. Make the best use of what you've got. Again, this may mean moving things around a few times until they're stored in the best place. It takes some trial and error, but it's definitely worth doing some experimentation for this is process. Because if it frees up space and clutter in the areas you access every single day, it will definitely make life easier.

And I know you're all about that.

Off-Season Clothing

Maybe you're blessed to live in an area of the country (or the world) that doesn't require changing weights and types of clothing four times a year. Here in Ohio, we cycle through them all— sometimes all in the span of a few weeks. It's nuts, and it means we need a little more stuff to get through the change of seasons comfortably. Most often, that means different wardrobes for different seasons.

But even with four different seasons, that means that I'm wearing the same type of clothing for at least three months in a row. So why would I store items in my closet that I won't be wearing until nine months down the line? They're just cluttering up one of my most-used spaces nine months of the year. To solve this, we created seasonal clothing bins for each family member. It doesn't need to be labeled for the season. Whatever season we're currently in, that clothing lives in our spaces. The rest remains in the bin until the seasons change. Then, when the weather changes, we take the new season's items out and put the opposite season's items back in. It frees up room in our dressers and closets, is easy to access, and doesn't require some complicated system.

Sounds simple, works like a dream. Don't you wish everything was like that?

Paper Storage

Life comes with a lot of paper. Mail, keepsakes and mementos, schoolwork....it's a lot. If you can find a system to store it all that works for you, it'll eliminate a ton of the daily clutter that ends up living on our kitchen tables and countertops, office desks, and other hot spot drop zones at home. What's my method? Each piece immediately gets a home.

When our mail comes daily, packages are unpacked and envelopes are opened. Anything unneeded goes in the recycling or the trash, and the rest gets sorted out and put into its place. The key to having everything in its place? A really good system.

We have four hanging file folders on our kitchen wall that do most of the dirty work. They've made life with kids easier and eliminated missed bill payments, forgetting to return school permission slips, and added kitchen countertop clutter. Any paper that comes into our home goes into one of four folders: Action Items, To File, Keepsake Storage, or the Outbox.

Action Items are anything that requires a signature, a payment, or something to be done. Maybe it's a mortgage refinancing offer my husband and I need to discuss or a bill for a medical visit. Perhaps it's a form that needs to be signed for school. Whatever it is, it lives in that folder, and seeing it reminds me every time I pass by that something needs to be done. When we've paid that bill, it gets moved to the To File folder. When we've signed that form and it's ready to go back to school, it goes to the Outbox folder. No longer needed? It gets shredded or recycled—easy and simple.

What goes in To File? It's copies of a birth certificate that came in the mail, a paper copy of a medical bill that's recently been paid, or a tax document or refund check copy that needs to be kept for financial reasons. Any paper that needs to be kept around goes into our office files or gets scanned into the computer and then recycled or shredded.

How about Keepsake Storage? That's the folder for the sentimental handprint art that our preschooler brings home, our first grader's school picture, and maybe the hospital band from our baby's birth. Although we're pretty minimal as far as the items we keep, I do like to hold onto the most sentimental ones—the big moments, the photos, the tiny handprint masterpieces—and file them away for our kids to rifle through later. As for the rest, I'll snap a photo and add it to our online photo albums so the kids will be able to see some of their precious works of art without being handed file boxes of physical projects twenty years from now. They'll still get a glimpse into their childhood without the physical burden of bins full of stuff.

Outbox is pretty self-explanatory. Maybe it's a wedding invitation RSVP that needs to be mailed, a signed homework project that needs to go back to school, or even a too-small T-shirt to be passed down to a niece or nephew. It's a place to keep items that need to leave our home without cluttering up countertops, and it's as easy as can be.

This is a system I've created after years of trial and error. It works for me and our home, and it may work for yours—or maybe it won't. The only way to find the system that works best for you is to try them out. Tweak ones that you find out there. Create your own. Do what works for you and your family. Just make sure it's simple, because an overly complicated system isn't going to serve you much better than no system at all.

CHAPTER 12

Simpler Boundaries

Let's talk about boundaries. They're essential for real life, and virtual life isn't any different. Whether it's social media, email, texts, or phone calls, it's so important to realize that it's unhealthy (and unrealistic) to make ourselves available all the time. And it's even unhealthier to make ourselves available just because someone else wants us to be.

Whether it's the call from your friend that you just don't have the emotional bandwidth to handle, the work email that comes after hours and interrupts your peaceful dinner with your family, or the always-present alerts from your Facebook or Instagram calling for you to respond to a comment, like, or message, none of those "calls" are essential, especially if they pull you away from better things happening right there in front of you. Learn to say no—often. Because none of that is essential; none of it needs to be done right this minute, especially if it steals your time and energy away from things you'd rather be doing. Prioritize the things that are more important to you; things that fill your cup, light you up, and make your life more joyful.

It's easy to get sucked into the world of everyone else's needs. It's easy to be distracted by an alert on Instagram, only to find yourself still mindlessly scrolling half an hour later. It's so easy to say yes to that last-minute request for baked goods for the school bake sale. We fool ourselves into responding to these calls because we tell ourselves a story that it's *all* important. But is it really? The more that we convince ourselves that it's always essential to respond to all this clamor for our attention, the more we pull ourselves away from the present and get sucked into a world where we're functioning in response to what's coming from the *outside*, rather than dictating what's important from the *inside*.

When we get it all done—respond to everyone's requests and multitask ourselves into oblivion based on the needs of others—we wear it like a badge of honor. But all that badge earns us is lost time, lost energy, and lost joy.

I know because I used to be there. I used to say yes to *everyone* so I never disappointed *anyone*. I devoted my energy to responding to the demands of the outside world. I handed off my valuable time to the highest bidder—usually the person or thing that screamed the loudest for it. I gave when it was asked of me, regardless of whether I had anything to give.

And I was absolutely miserable. Instead of feeling good for responding to everyone else's needs, I was beyond drained. I was angry, I was resentful, and I absolutely felt taken advantage of even though I had been the one who had said yes to every request that came along.

Sound familiar? It's a common theme in motherhood and a trap that many of us fall into. It's critically important to take care of our family, but it's important to take care of ourselves, too. It's essential to learn to prioritize our own needs first to get what we need to be able to be the best version of ourselves. Sure, there will be days that pull energy from us as well as days when emergencies crop up and we need to function in a more responsive way. But if most days feel like you're responding to what's happening with your world and your family rather than consciously determining where your time and energy go, you're setting yourself up to be disappointed, frustrated, and stressed out.

Let go of the self-imposed rules that to be a good and successful person, you have to say yes to everything. *You don't.* In fact, the more you establish boundaries, and the more you learn to say no to things that don't align with the way you'd like to spend your minutes, hours and days, the more you'll appreciate what you're doing with your time. If you've been saying yes to everyone and everything, this will be hard. You'll feel like you're letting people down. You'll swear that you're dropping the ball. But you'll also gain back more of what you *want* to do with your time—more of what fills your cup, accomplishes your own goals, and feeds your soul. Eventually, those boundaries will begin to feel more like walls that keep the good things in rather than barricades that keep the bad things out.

SET YOUR BOUNDARIES

Boundaries aren't a line in the sand; they're not selfish, and they're certainly not permanent. They will bend, flex, and even completely change based on the season of life you're in. But they are necessary because they set you up for happiness. They're decisions you're making to prioritize your mental health. They're a promise you're making to yourself to put your own needs, wants, and happiness at the top of the list, not because the rest of life isn't important, but because *you* are important, too.

What I need and what I can give changes daily. Some days, I've gotten the sleep I need; my energy levels are high, and I'm able to get what I need done. I'm happy to give more freely to others when that happens—to say yes to reading more books, joining more tea parties, and building more Lego towers. I have more time and energy to let a friend vent about their horrible week and can contribute genuine time and energy to listening and responding without feeling burdened by their needs. I've got extra time on my hands to help others without feeling weighed down with obligation—all because I've *chosen* to volunteer my time and energy.

There are also days where I'm hitting a low. The baby was up all night, the toddler is having constant tantrums, the kids are bickering yet again, and there's not enough coffee in the world. It's also probably only 8:00 a.m., and I know that I'm already riding on empty. These are the days I learn to say no to almost everything. I cancel any nonessential commitments, I put off my to-do list for another day, and I spend time refueling my tank. That may mean ordering in dinner, watching way too much Disney+, and letting dirty dishes pile up in the sink.

That's okay, because tomorrow is another day to do things differently. And most of the time, I'm recharged after a day of lounging and doing the bare minimum. I'm alive, the kids are alive, and we've gotten through a tough day in a gentler, more enjoyable way, with what will hopefully be a better day on the horizon.

Establishing boundaries looks different for everyone, but there are some easy ways I've found that give me the ability to do it in a gentle way. Do you know what is almost always involved? Saying no. Healthy boundaries mean saying no to a commitment or invitation if it doesn't serve me, and can also include saying no to a task even though I have the time or capability to do it. And taking care of myself requires me to say no to a relationship that asks a lot of me and doesn't provide anything in return.

A SIMPLER MOTHERHOOD

Boundaries are necessary, because it's your life, not anyone else's. And at the end of it, no one's going to be handing out prizes for getting the most things done. You won't win any awards for being the most tired, or the most stressed. You won't be getting accolades because you only slept five hours a night, or worked sixty hours a week, or kept your house perfectly clean and put together every single day.

Remember, if *everything* is important, *nothing* is important. Prioritize you. You only have one life, and *you* determine what that's filled with. You get a say in how the story is written. You choose how your days are lived. Don't look back and regret where you invested your time, because at the end of the day, it's your most valuable resource. Once it's spent, you can't get it back.

MAKE YOUR SMARTPHONE SMART

Technology is an amazing thing. In today's world, it provides us with unlimited sources of connectivity, information, and entertainment. It allows us to be able to reach people and do all kinds of other things twenty-four hours a day, seven days a week, 365 days a year. For most of us, that functionality is all contained in a piece of metal, glass, and plastic that fits in the palm of our hand. Pretty amazing, right?

Until it isn't. Because let's face it—having all that power at our disposal at all times can also be a huge burden. It can weigh us down, distract us from what's going on right in front of our eyes, and saddle us with guilt. It can pull our attention away from the present and suck us into a virtual world of comparison where nothing is good enough and everyone is happier, thinner, and more successful than we are. Most importantly, it can rob us of valuable time with its constant chirps, dings, beeps, and flashing notifications. If we're not careful, it can remove us from the life we've worked so hard to create for ourselves and tear away all the good that real life has to offer—and in its place, it often leaves nothing but time wasted on things that just aren't as important.

So how do you avoid that? I simplify my phone by removing everything that doesn't bring value. I delete unnecessary apps. I remove notifications. I usually keep my phone on silent. Most often, I lay my phone face down on a counter or table out of reach. The lure of that phone lighting up with any number of alerts is just too great. In fact, tech companies do extensive research to find ways to lure you into using your phone. Colorful alerts, dinging sounds, and flashing notifications—they're all designed to be as addictive and appealing as possible. Don't fall into the trap.

There are so many ways to curb your phone usage—apps that measure your time, and limits you can set in your settings. But I find it easiest to physically remove the temptation altogether: out of sight, out of mind. It's too easy to mindlessly pick up my phone when it's within reach and get sucked into nothing important, only to find myself still scrolling or googling as much as an hour later. Don't be passive with your time, take control of it. If you know you're not able to resist all the notifications and beeps, silence and remove them. If you know having your phone in sight or within reach is still too tempting, put it face down in the other room. There's a realistic and simple way to make sure your phone serves you as a useful tool rather than a life-diminishing distraction: Just don't give it a starring role in your home in the first place.

SIMPLIFY THAT SOCIAL MEDIA

I understand the complete and utter irony of a blogger writing about simplifying social media. I created my Instagram blog years ago as a way to have my own little side project—an outlet to do something I enjoy and share a message I'm passionate about with a little corner of the world. As my audience rapidly grew, I quickly learned that social media can absolutely take over your life. Whether you've got fifteen followers or 50,000, social media can pull you away from the real and suck you into the highlight reel of everyone else's. And it took a lot of trial and error for me to learn how to simplify when it came to the actual tool I was using to get my message out to the world. But I managed to discover some pretty simple ways to find the balance between enjoying social media and becoming a slave to it. So here I am, about to share with you some easy ways to find the balance between utilizing it as a tool...or bearing it as a burden.

Turn Down the Distraction

What would our lives look like if we never saw so much of everyone else's? Online posts show us their homes, their décor, their wardrobes, and their organized pantries; what their kids ate for dinner; the way they arranged their playroom; and the DIY project they spent the weekend doing that totally transformed their kitchen. It's a beautiful thing to be able to share your life with the world, but it's also only a tiny snippet of reality. And for some reason, it's easier to believe that the highlight reel you're scrolling through of everyone else's reality is the whole picture. Guess what? It's not.

I am all for using social media for entertainment, motivation, and community. It's an absolutely fabulous tool...when it's used the right way, at the right times, and when you're in the right frame of mind to keep it in perspective. Outside of that context, it can easily become a depressing, isolating time suck that does nothing for your productivity and simply further removes you from the life you've worked so hard to fashion for yourself.

When it comes to social media, much of how you feel about yourself and your life follows the same law of diminishing returns that the rest of the good things in life follow: A great thing is great... but only in moderation. What's the easiest way I've found to curb my social media habit? Delete the distraction.

Whether it's mindlessly scrolling your Instagram feed, responding to comments and messages, or getting sucked into video after video on Facebook, it's easiest to remove the distraction from your phone altogether. By deleting the app, I'm no longer tempted to pop on for a quick minute and get roped into spending more time on my phone than I planned. It takes two minutes to redownload the app when I'm ready to use it again, and it redirects my focus to things in real life—you know, the stuff that really matters at the end of the day.

And I'll be honest, I don't realize how mindlessly I reach for my phone as a distraction until I delete those little brightly colored squares from my home screen. I'm instantly made aware of how ridiculously often I tend to reach for it once that little app is absent. It's often the reality check that I need to shift my focus to things that are going on right now, in the present, rather than distracting myself with cheap, easy, and addictive entertainment.

It also allows me to realize once more how much "free" time I really have. Without the distraction of apps shoving exciting stories, addictive videos, and beautiful photos in my face throughout the day, I find I've got much more time on my hands than I thought to do more intentional, fulfilling things. I find there *is* time to take a walk around the neighborhood, or go on a trip to the playground. Tackling that extra load of laundry suddenly feels more possible, not to mention reorganizing that kitchen cabinet that's been driving me nuts lately. With less social media time, I'm able to do things like read a chapter of a good book, take time to really play with my kids, or just sit and relax with absolutely nothing to do but breathe and invite a little more calm into my day. All of these things are in my opinion far more meaningful than the passive entertainment of social media. So you may want to consider this option.

You Are What You Consume

It's a clichéd saying, but it goes for just about everything in life. It's not just what you put into your body on a daily basis; it's about what you feed your mind, heart, and soul, too. It's where you spend your time, and it's the people and messages you allow to become a part of your life. It's about making sure you're intentionally choosing who and what you're including in your day-to-day experience.

Social media is no different. You have a choice about whether to welcome all that content into your life. You get to choose whose messages are coming through, what types of messages you're seeing, and how that content is making you feel. You get a say in how often you're letting other people's lives entertain and influence you (because let's face it, there's a very good reason why social media rock stars are called "influencers"). I'm not saying all of this to scare you, but rather to make you aware of this reality and to allow you to reorient your perspective to one of active, intentional choice rather than being passively influenced.

Setting limits on your time on social media is great. Being selective as to who you follow is even better. And making sure that the content you're receiving is not viewed as the end-all, be-all source of your news and information consumption is the very best. After all, social media began as a way to connect—a form of virtual social entertainment. And although it's grown and evolved over the years, it shouldn't be the only way you gather information about the world around you. The accounts you follow and the people you listen to may be experts in their field, but they're out there to share just one small viewpoint in this vast world. You can use your time on social media to contribute to your community, connect with others, disseminate information, and entertain yourself and your audience. But remember that with power comes responsibility, and it is your responsibility to use that power (both for yourself and for others) wisely.

Be selective in the feeds you curate, the content you produce, and the messages you're sending and receiving. Be mindful of the time you spend creating and consuming content, the extent to which you let it pervade your life, and the way you feel afterwards. Social media should make you feel more connected, more informed, and more entertained, as well as more motivated, more encouraged, and more hopeful. If the people and messages you're consuming aren't doing that for you on a daily basis, simply unfollow. Disconnect. Go find sources of happiness in your life that provide those for you.

You only get one life. Surround yourself with the vibes you want.

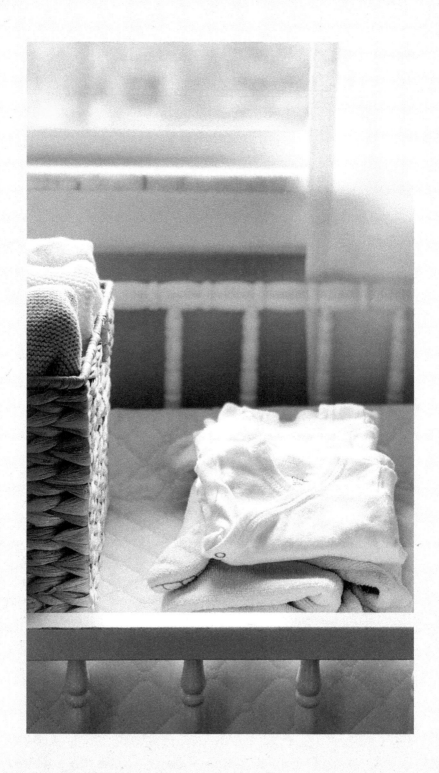

CHAPTER 13

Simpler Parenting

It wouldn't be a book on motherhood if we didn't sit down and chat about how to simplify parenting, right? Because being a mom is hard—like, really hard. The universal truth is that all of us had to learn to be mothers. None of us were born into motherhood; it is a hard-earned title for every single mother on this planet. Does that make you feel a bit better about your imperfect parenting? It should. Being a good parent is completely subjective, and it looks a bit different for every single one of us. But there's also some pretty universal end goals when it comes to parenting, and I'm pretty sure one of those is to make things a bit simpler. And I'm here to help.

Please know that simpler parenting isn't perfect parenting. It isn't effortless parenting. And there certainly isn't a one-stop, follow-this-regimen, one-size-fits-all solution. Because we're all different—our kids, our homes, our lifestyles, our values are all different. Therefore, finding your way when it comes to simpler parenting isn't going to happen if you're only making tweaks to behaviors, environments, and responses. The real change is comes from learning to accept your unique parenthood journey and embracing it, exactly as it is. Because being a parent is quite possibly one of the biggest privileges and positions of power we can be given as human beings.

When I stopped working and decided to become a stay-at-home mom over six years ago, I really struggled with my identity. I felt like I did nothing but cook, clean, change diapers, make to-do lists, clean up toys, and de-escalate tantrums—over and over again, every day. Wash, rinse, repeat. It was then that I made the conscious decision that my role as a mother was far more than maintaining a home and keeping my kids alive. Decluttering and simplifying was the first step to removing the noise in my daily life so I could pour my attention, energy, and love into the members of my family. But it didn't solve all my problems. I also had to get my heart right, too.

Because unmade beds can wait in the morning. But those little, open hearts just waiting to be molded and filled with love and kindness—they can't. They want my undivided attention. They deserve it. And as I've simplified my heart and my head over the years, I've come to realize something: They *need* it.

It's a crazy world out there right now. And if the past year or so has taught me anything, it's that as a parent, I wield immeasurable power in deciding the outcome of our future. These little people are going to become adults in the next few decades, and it is my responsibility to raise kind, inclusive, openhearted and open-minded children. It is my job to create a home environment that's built on a strong foundation of love. It's my job to focus my priorities on spending my time raising my kids, not maintaining my things. All that other noise? It can wait. Being a mom comes first.

Are you ready? Good. It's time to roll up our sleeves and get to work.

EMBRACE YOUR SEASON

What season of motherhood are you in? Maybe you're deep in the trenches of midnight feedings with your first baby. Or you're struggling with managing a crawling babe and a whiny toddler. Maybe your kids are all returning home from a day of school, answering your questions with one-word answers, simple snorts... or complete silence. Perhaps you're getting ready to send that oldest one off to college and wondering where the heck these last eighteen years went. Regardless of where you are, I bet you'd love to find more moments of simple joy in your day—who wouldn't? Want to know one of the easiest ways to find joy in parenting? Acknowledge the season of motherhood you're in and own it. Because it's just that: a season.

Maybe it's that utterly gutting newborn sleep deprivation; the daily, epically loud toddler tantrums; and the constant train wreck of toys littering your playroom floor at all hours of the day. Perhaps it's the nonstop stream of poop, fart, and butt jokes polluting your ears daily, or the nonstop backtalk, the refusal to help with anything, the constant attitude, and the exclamations of "You're the worst mom ever!" as they stomp out of the room. It could be a complete lack of communication altogether, possibly along with their disregard for curfew and nonstop trips to the grocery store to fill the fridge for what feels like the fifteenth time this week, without so much as a "Thanks, mom." Regardless of the stage of motherhood you're currently in, each season has its struggles. So start giving yourself grace.

The house won't always be clutter-free. The fridge won't always be stocked. The pantry won't always be organized. The dishes won't always be put away. The kids won't always behave. The laundry won't always be done. The dinner won't always be healthy and homemade. The kids won't always be clean. Heck, *you* won't always be clean—and that's okay.

Because if it means that you're able to let go of your expectations and soak in all those good moments of motherhood—you know, the everyday ones that somehow imprint themselves on your heart and fill your soul—it's worth all the imperfect, undone things around you. Years from now, those sticky kitchen floors or that perfectly tidied linen closet and Pinterest-worthy playroom shelf—none of that will matter. But all those memories of your seasons of motherhood sure will. Don't miss the beauty of the season while it's here, right in front of you.

What does embracing your season look like? It means taking things off your plate when you're overwhelmed or stressed. It means learning to say no to invitations, expectations, and events that aren't realistic for where you are in your life. Basically, it means letting go of trying to do it all, and it means saying yes to the things that matter at the stage of motherhood you're in. Those could be blanket forts, another push on the swing, saying yes to having friends over for a sleepover, or some one-on-one time with the kid who's really struggling right now.

I'm all for finding routines and rhythms that work for your stage of life. But keep in mind that things change often in motherhood. Just when your kid says they like macaroni, they're refusing it the very next day. Right when you think your toddler is sleeping through the night, they'll be up five times with nightmares. It's totally reasonable to work at achieving goals that aid in the happiness of you and your children. But it's also reasonable to remember that nothing is black and white when it comes to kids, and you should prepare to have to adjust and make changes to accommodate your season, your child, and your own sanity.

If you're in the season of baby making, baby carrying, and baby having: big sigh. I know; minimalism and babies can surely feel like one huge contradiction. But it's only temporary.

Those pump parts and the bottles littering the sink, countertops, and drying rack will be gone in a flash, and that newborn baby will be asking for some more water in their sippy cup before you know it. That baby swing, those baby carriers, and that fully stuffed diaper bag will soon they'll be replaced by towers of blocks, requests to be put down, and a smaller purse full of half-melted fruit snacks and cracker crumbs. All those bins of baby clothing in different sizes? In a year or two, they'll be packed into shopping bags and passed out the front door into the appreciative hands of a sister or a friend with tear-filled eyes and a nostalgic heart as your toddler naps quietly in their big kid bed.

All that baby stuff sure can feel like a frustrating amount of clutter sometimes. But it's the best kind of clutter—the fleeting kind. It's the kind that reminds you that those babies grow up all too quickly. In essence, it serves to challenge your need to have things your way, as well as reminding you that motherhood is about compromise and sacrifice. It's a process that's so much bigger than just you and what you'd like your home (and your individual life) to be. The inevitable chaos when your children are very little is, in a sense, there to help you remember that a home is meant to be lived in and those babies are meant to be loved on.

That baby clutter won't last forever, and neither will those baby years. Soak it all in, find peace with the chaos, and lock that fleeting clutter and all the wonderfulness that comes with it in your heart forever.

STOP CHASING PLAYROOM PERFECTION

Motherhood is so much easier when there's an order to your stuff. But don't mistake order for perfection.

I fought the good fight for years, wanting pretty, perfectly matching bins to hide all the clutter and color in our playroom. I longed for a seamlessly coordinated space that kept all the stuff out of sight. I dreamed of piles of wooden toys stacked neatly on cube shelving, and woven baskets concealing any trace of mess in my home. So I went out and bought all the storage cubes and baskets, and I did my best to perfectly organize toys by type. I drove myself absolutely bonkers recreating rooms I'd seen splashed all over Instagram and Pinterest, hoping that they'd make me a happier mom. Instead, all I ended up with was a huge pile of messes after those large, pretty, woven bins got dumped out in search of a specific brightly colored singing toy.

Listen, it's okay to have a beautifully styled playroom. But it's also totally okay if you don't. It's all right if the toys aren't all hidden and concealed, or wooden and color-coordinating, lined up in rainbow order, or the newest and "trendiest." In our home, we've got action figures with arms missing that are still well-loved and constantly played with every day, a hodgepodge of secondhand doll clothes and toys, and a collection of repurposed Lego sets missing a few pieces. All you need is a simple system to keep things organized and encourage independent play. If you want to make it a picture-perfect, coordinating playroom because that is something that will give you pleasure, do it.

But if you don't want to, that's okay, too. It's *their* playroom, with *their* toys in it. If they're loved and played with, let the toys stay. Let it be imperfect, and be satisfied with that. Come up with simple solutions to get the toys up off the floor at the end of each day, and then move on to more important things. It's just toy storage—nothing more, nothing less. Find a system that works for you and your kids and go with it.

Then get down and make messes with them, because there's going to come a day when there won't be any more brightly colored play kitchens and piled baskets of superheroes, or any more messes at all, and you're going to miss it. Enjoy the beautiful chaos while it's there, right in front of you. It's a reminder of all the life lived in that space daily.

LET THEM BE MESSY

I spent years trying to keep the toys from exploding all over the house. I tried every organizational system out there. I used the easiest bins, cubbies, and hooks I could find for storing all their items. I used a toy rotation system and constantly edited the toys my children had out and available. I cleaned up throughout the day so their playroom didn't absolutely drive me nuts.

All that was well and good, but it didn't solve my problem: The kids still made messes, and I still spent all the time in the world chasing behind them in an effort to keep things manageable. Eventually, I succumbed to the disorder, and news flash: Nobody died. And I learned that it was okay for their play space to be messy—in fact, it was necessary. Creativity and imaginative play require a little mess. It's what childhood is all about, really.

So now, our playroom is the one space in our home where simplicity doesn't always reign. Don't get me wrong—I still love a good simple system to store our toys. I love rotating their things in and out of storage as the kids grow and their interests change, and I almost always do one big dance party cleanup at the end of every day with the little ones to ensure a fresh start for the next day.

Bring on the big bins of endless Lego pieces, and the messy paints and Play-Doh. Let the mess sit during the day as they actually use the space. Prioritize a playroom that sparks creativity and encourages their imaginations. But most importantly, do what works best for you. If a perpetually clean play area is your priority, keep it tidy. If a mess drives you insane, a midday clean-up is absolutely fine. But let me also give you permission to let go during the day as they explore, learn, and play. A simple life is just as much about letting go of the expectations you have for yourself and your home as it is about letting go of your physical stuff.

Let them be messy. Control your urge to tidy up their creations for the sake of your own needs. After all, it's their space. It'll get picked up eventually. Enjoy the chaos and let them be kids. It'll make things infinitely easier, save your time and sanity, and let your kiddos know that imperfection is okay, too.

FIND THAT BALANCE

When it comes to parenting (and really, anything else in life), we can't be experts at everything. We're all complex human beings, capable of growing, learning, and evolving. As parents, I think that means being able to straddle both sides of the parenting line.

I don't think any of us were meant to be confined to a tidy little box. It's okay to see both sides of a parenting issue, to change your mind, or (heaven forbid) to create your own answer.

- You can be a minimalist and still allow your kids to find immense joy in their things.
- You can pride yourself on your advanced education and still allow your kids to binge-watch *Blippi*.
- You can find value in wooden and educational toys but still also buy your kids the bright, colorful, plastic ones that make lots of sounds and require batteries.
- You can enjoy a tidy home and still choose to let your six-year-old leave his bed unmade.
- You can buy organic groceries for your family and still treat your kids to Happy Meals.
- You can love shopping sustainably but still buy your toddler those five-dollar T-shirts from Target because you know they'll be destroyed in a season.
- You can be on a budget but also splurge for a drive-through pumpkin spice latte and cake pops for your passengers.
- You can be present for your kiddos and still enjoy some mindless Instagram scrolling in your downtime.
- You can use cloth diapers for your baby yet also keep some disposables around for those days when you just can't take it.

Don't let the world tell you that you have to choose a lane on every issue under the sun when it comes to parenting and stay in it, because you don't. Don't let them make you believe that you must pick a side to every facet of motherhood. You can live in both camps, and (dare I say) enjoy parts of each.

Courageously chase after the motherhood that brings you and your children happiness, and stop trying to fit into a perfect little box. Choose to create a home for your children that makes you proud—as messy, complex, and undefinable as that may be. Go color outside the lines. Venture into new territory. Try something scary and new, and see what it adds to your life.

Because I think motherhood—and life, too—is a far more beautiful world when we do.

THE KIDS COME FIRST

Confession: I used to prioritize a clean home above my kids. It makes my stomach churn just thinking about how many times I declined requests to play because I was too busy with a cleaning task that "had" to be completed. I let my type A nature get the best of me and spent hour after hour jumping from one project to the next. I'd heave a huge sigh when my kids dropped crumbs on my freshly mopped floor. I spent too much time on my phone, searching for the latest cleaning routine or method that would finally restore permanent order in my home.

Except nothing did.

And then I got my priorities straight, which isn't an easy thing for a perfectionist like me. It's taken a lot of conscious effort on my part to reframe my life as a stay-at-home mom, and it now includes a lot more emphasis on the mom part—and a lot less on the perfect home end of things.

Some days, my home is pretty tidy. Some days, I get a burst of energy and tackle a chunk of cleaning projects while the kids play independently. And I absolutely do stress when my home is in shambles due to a stomach bug, a tough week at school, or life. But then I let it go, because there will be plenty of time in my life to have a perfectly clean home. But these four children of mine? They won't be little for long. It's taken a lot of effort on my part, but I now catch myself when my priorities tip too far off the right path. I now spend most of my days playing and interacting with and loving on those four. I don't regret a minute of it.

Those kids come first. They're the most important part of your daily work. Whether you stay at home or work full-time, if there's only one thing you accomplish today, make it this: Get down and play with your kids.

Because tonight, when they lay their heads down on their pillows and close those tired little eyes, reflecting on their day, they won't be grateful for those clean kitchen floors you spent an hour mopping. They're unlikely to appreciate that perfectly organized pantry you put together after hours of denying their requests to "Watch!" or that expertly curated meal plan you crafted instead of cuddling up on the couch. They'll be most grateful that you played with them.

And I bet you will, too.

FAILING IS NORMAL

I wish someone would have told me that I'd learn the most as a mom from my failures—that getting it wrong was as important as getting it right. I wish they'd clued me in that in order to become the best mother to my children, I'd go through so many days where I felt like I had no idea what I was doing, that I'd question and overanalyze every decision I ever made: breastfeeding, sleep training, diapers, nap schedules, baby wearing, pacifiers—I'd overthink it all.

I wish someone would have let me know that I'd have days where I did nothing more than keep them alive, that I'd spend countless nights awake at three in the morning, feeling guilty for raising my voice in anger and frustration at these tiny little people, or that I'd cry from embarrassment on the way home from the grocery store after dragging an angry toddler out kicking and screaming, with all eyes on me.

I wish someone would have told me that no "must have" item would solve all my problems; that I'd have to try six different types of swaddles before I found the right one, or that I'd be buying every bottle on the market before my child would finally accept one. I wish they'd said to me that I'd end up with a drawer full of beautiful, untouched baby outfits while my little one would live in the same five zip-up sleepers.

But even if someone *had* told me all this, I wish I would have listened, because I probably wouldn't have. Motherhood is one big learning curve, failure after failure after failure. You learn what to do, sure. But more often than not, you learn what *not* to do, because no one can tell you how to grow into the woman your children need. Those tiny little beings are uniquely yours, sent to your arms with the purpose of helping you figure out who you are and what you need to be for them.

Embrace those failures. Pay attention. Don't waste your time chasing after perfection and bashing yourself for the errors of your ways. Instead, take those failures as signs pointing you in the right direction; steering you onto the path you need to take to become the mother you were destined to be. The minute you can see all those failures as growing pains, that's the minute this simpler motherhood thing becomes possible. When you let go of the reins and allow failure, imperfection, and mistakes to enter your mothering experience, that's when your motherhood starts feeling like one big, beautiful grace-filled blessing.

NORMALIZE GOOD ENOUGH

I get it: It's super easy to scroll through social media, flip on the TV, and even drive through your neighborhood and instantly feel less-than. As a woman and a mother in our society today, it's ingrained in us, this constant need to do better, be better, have better. Don't get me wrong—wanting to be a great mother, wife, and friend is a beautiful thing. It drives us to chase after our dreams, grow as individuals, and strive to get the most out of our lives.

But when the quest for "better" becomes a constant in our lives, it's no longer serving us. When better becomes an unyielding chase after only the best, it robs us of all the contentment, joy, and pride that the here and now is offering up. It clutters our mind with a constant to-do list—a consuming sense of inadequacy—and it steals precious moments of time from our seasons of motherhood that we can't ever get back.

But do you want to know something incredible? That race—that constant competition to be better that every mom seems to be entering? It's an optional one. You can choose to join in or opt out. The decision is completely yours.

Me? I stepped out of that race years ago, and I'm never going back. I'm okay over here with my imperfect children, who sometimes throw tantrums in public, don't sleep through the night, and clutter our home with their blanket forts, favorite toys, and vivid imaginations—especially if it means living a life of less yelling, nagging, and crying (on both my part and the kids').

I'm okay with my half home-cooked meals, my half-organic grocery list, and my half-clean bathrooms—especially if it means more time to read a book with my kids, play a game of tag, or take a walk on a beautiful, sunny day.

I'm okay with off-brand gym shoes, wrinkled shirts, and store-bought birthday cakes if it means more muddy puddle jumping, less laundry folding, and a magical homemade birthday my kiddos won't ever forget.

Because it's a good enough motherhood for me. It's far from perfect, but it serves me and my family. Accepting this makes room in my head and heart to be able to stop and live in the moment most days, room to get down and play with my kids, to pause and actually listen to them, and to sit and soak in this beautiful motherhood that for years, I only dreamed of having,

Listen, I'm not here to preach to you about my "arrival" to a season of blissful motherhood. Nor am I here to feed into the spiraling world of #momlife memes. Instead, I'm simply choosing to exist somewhere in the middle. I'm here to embrace all of it—the good and the bad. Every day I'm choosing to find that ever-elusive balance of expectation and reality, and to squeeze absolutely every wonderful drop out of this fleeting season of life while I can. And when it comes to parenting, that means making their time a priority.

Because being a mom is a pretty awesome gift. And I don't want to waste it worrying about being perfect.

CHAPTER 14

Writing Your Own Simple Story

I'm currently sitting here on my cozy living room couch, typing away on my keyboard as our three-month-old sleeps in the swing. My husband is perched in the armchair across the room, pensively eyeing his laptop screen as he works from home. Our oldest is back from a long day at school, playing quietly with Legos in his room as he decompresses from a long week. My girls, now four and two, stand staring intently, dangerously close to the TV, as *Mickey Mouse Clubhouse* keeps them glued to the screen. The sink is full of dishes; the floor is littered with toys, empty snack bowls, and baby-containing contraptions. Things are far from the picture-perfect reality you probably envision when you imagine my life.

Yet my heart has never been fuller. In a few hours, I'll fire up the oven for our weekly Friday Night Pizza tradition. The kids will eagerly await the ding of the timer. The house will fill with the familiar smell of rising dough and warm, melting cheese. I'll sit on the couch, glass of wine in hand, and smile tiredly at my husband as we catch up on our hopes and dreams for a few short minutes—and I'll know, with all certainty, that these moments will remain forever etched in my mind and across my heart when I'm old and grey.

Because years from now, I'll remember the freedom of the space in our lives. I'll reflect on the magical messes that will soon be a distant memory. I'll remember the lightness in my heart, even at the hardest, heaviest times, that only existed because I learned to let go of the wheel and let life play out as it was destined to do within the four walls of this home.

Life is messy, and imperfect, and out of our hands most days. But when we learn to let go of the things that don't serve us and instead focus on those that do, we quickly realize that things easily become simpler. When we remove the clutter of things that don't matter and clutch tightly to the strings of those that do, we are able to move forward and forge a beautiful life full of gratitude, contentment, and hope—and we take a whole lot less stuff along with us on the ride.

Now that I've shared my heart with you, it's time for you to write your own story—and it's easier than you think. Don't overcomplicate things, or dive into huge projects, or plan to overhaul your entire life for the sake of simplicity. Just follow your heart, do what feels right, and take the tips I've shared with you and use them to make small, daily changes that will add up to a life full of more space, joy, and contentment.

Because simple living isn't a destination; it's a constant journey. To put it simply, it's living intuitively. It is doing things as they're needed or feel right—making changes as life urges you to shift this way or that, rather than following someone else's program or schedule. It's making the choice, every day, to prioritize what matters, the decision to live out your minutes as you wish, rather than being told what to do. It's active engagement in your life rather than passive rule-following. It's a culmination of many actions; of changes, of edits to your home, your things, the way you think about life, and the way you choose to live it. If you tried to declutter, get out of debt, minimize, organize, and simplify every aspect of your life at once, you'd probably be overwhelmed. You'd feel defeated when major changes didn't immediately happen. And you'd probably give up.

Don't strive for instant change and get frustrated when things don't magically follow. The day you plant the seed is not the day you eat the fruit.

I know, it's the last thing you want to hear or believe, because this world tells you otherwise on the daily. Right around the corner, we are told, there's a quick fix for just about anything you could want. We're sold the idea every day that for the right price, the next life-changing solution can be yours; that within minutes, hours, or days, things can be infinitely better.

Except it won't be. Because all good things take time. You have to put in the work.

Give yourself the time and space it takes to make lasting change. Take it a drawer, a closet, or a cabinet at a time. Cross something off your calendar here; say no there. Stop spending hours searching for the perfect cleaning routines, and start spending minutes running the vacuum when the mood strikes. Stop researching the best ways to raise your children, and start getting down and playing with them. Stop trying to curate the perfect capsule wardrobe, and start hanging only items that you love in your closet.

And know that all those small changes will add up a life that is fuller, yet emptier; a life full of joy, space, time, energy, peace, and contentment; a life of less comparison, debt, stress, self-doubt, and clutter. It's a simple balancing game—adding a little of the best stuff in and removing a little of the not-so-great, one day, one item, one task at a time.

A simpler life can be yours, but it isn't going to happen over-night—nor after one ruthless, rage-fueled decluttering session. It won't happen after a long weekend of purging the basement, nor following an expensive shopping spree for all the best organizing products and solutions.

The day you plant the seed isn't the day your life will change.

But it will be the day an incredible journey begins.

Let the Journey Begin

A simple motherhood isn't an easy one—let's get that straight.

Even a simple life is a real one. Real life is messy and cluttered, stressful and hard. Beds don't get made. Counters get cluttered. Kids get sick. Coffee gets spilled. Even the simplest, most organized home has its share of messes.

But what a simple life provides is this: Contentment. Peace, hope, and grace. Acceptance. It's a life that *feels* simple, a life that affords you the time to get down and play with your toddlers and to rock that baby a few extra minutes before bedtime. It allows you to look past the small messes and the to-do lists and to redirect your time toward the people in your life, not the things.

I started my journey to a simpler motherhood so that these days wouldn't just pass me by. When I became a mother, I struggled with devoting all my time to taking care of my things while overlooking what really mattered: all those magical, everyday moments with my little people. I was tired of the "Just a minute!" and "When I'm finished!" and "Can you *just* hold on!?" that my little ones heard from me on repeat. I was tired of feeling like I was treading water; like if I could just get everything done, *then* I'd be able to partake in my life. I didn't want to just survive motherhood—I wanted to thrive at it. I didn't want to always be so busy *maintaining* my life that I never took the time to *live* it.

I want you to know that right now, who you are and where you're at is *exactly enough*.

We know those dishes need to be washed. The toilets need to be scrubbed. We know the kids need another snack and that basement storage room needs to be organized.

Guess what? There will *always* be something to do, and a simpler life won't change that. But it sure will change how your *feel* about that mess; that mile-long list of chores; that endless mountain of laundry. It will provide you with the grace to accept that reality, to prioritize it in the right way, and often, to tell it to take a hike while you enjoy a hot cup of coffee or a good belly laugh with your children. That grace will allow you to table the nonessential for later while you immerse yourself in those everyday moments with your children that someday, will just be memories—to know in your heart, in your head, and deep in your soul that your time as a mother is a fleeting season. It is a time that merits the constant pursuit of all the best parts of life, experiences that, when stacked up together, help write your own beautiful, simple story.

Simple living has helped me find so much joy in my motherhood.

And my hope for you, my friend, is that these words of mine help you find the same.

ACKNOWLEDGEMENTS

Thank you to my readers, first and foremost, for welcoming me into your homes and your hearts to share my passion for a simpler life with you.

To my publisher, Mango Publishing, and Brenda Knight, who believed in me enough to provide me with the opportunity to share my message with the world.

Thank you to my children, Enzo, Halle, Ava, and Remi, for making me a mother and being the driving force for everything I do. You fill my life with so much joy, and I'm thankful every day that God gave me all of you.

To my husband, Nick: Thank you for encouraging me to chase after my dream, for changing countless dirty diapers while I poured my heart out onto these pages, and for always being in my corner. I couldn't do this parenthood thing without you.

And thank you to my parents for your lifelong support. Thanks to my dad, who taught me that hard work and a good attitude can get you anywhere in life; and to my mom, who created a magical childhood for all of us kids. Thank you for always making me feel loved and heard. You've always been my soft place to land.

ABOUT THE AUTHOR

Emily Eusanio is a mother of four and the creator of the popular Instagram account @the.simplified.mom, where she shares her experience living a life of less while navigating the chaos and clutter of motherhood. A reformed perfectionist and type A list maker extraordinaire, her mission is simple: to help moms everywhere find contentment, slow down, and make more room in their homes and hearts for the stuff that really matters. She lives in Cincinnati, Ohio, with her husband and four children.

Mango Publishing, established in 2014, publishes an eclectic list of books by diverse authors—both new and established voices—on topics ranging from business, personal growth, women's empowerment, LGBTQ studies, health, and spirituality to history, popular culture, time management, decluttering, lifestyle, mental wellness, aging, and sustainable living. We were recently named 2019 *and* 2020's #1 fastest-growing independent publisher by *Publishers Weekly*. Our success is driven by our main goal, which is to publish high-quality books that will entertain readers as well as make a positive difference in their lives.

Our readers are our most important resource; we value your input, suggestions, and ideas. We'd love to hear from you—after all, we are publishing books for you!

Please stay in touch with us and follow us at:

> Facebook: Mango Publishing
> Twitter: @MangoPublishing
> Instagram: @MangoPublishing
> LinkedIn: Mango Publishing
> Pinterest: Mango Publishing
> Newsletter: mangopublishinggroup.com/newsletter

Join us on Mango's journey to reinvent publishing, one book at a time.

CPSIA information can be obtained
at www.ICGtesting.com
Printed in the USA
JSHW012133180422
25057JS00010B/20